WILD WEST
Characters

by
Dale Pierce

Golden West Publishers

Front and back cover artwork by Cameron Daines

Unless otherwise credited, photos were taken by the author or are from the author's collection.

Library of Congress Cataloging-in-Publication Data

Pierce, Dale
  Wild West characters / by Dale Pierce.
  Includes index.
  1. West (U.S.)—History— 1848-1950—Biography.
I. Title.
F595.P6   1991   91-2039
920.078—dc20   CIP
ISBN 0-914846-53-1 (paperback)

Printed in the United States of America

Golden West Publishers   **(602) 265-4392**
4113 N. Longview Ave.
Phoenix, AZ 85014, USA

Contents

(continued on page 4)

Contents *(continued)*

Meet the Author . . . inside back cover

Introduction

While every effort to maintain a true profile of the various men and women depicted here has been made, it should be noted that history itself often proves an enemy, rather than a friend to the researcher.

Vital statistics — birthdates, and death notices — are sometimes nonexistent or conflicting. Accounts of incidents in books, newspaper articles, write-ups from publications at the time, and even court documents sometimes provide overlapping or distorted data which makes the task of turning out a project that vows to be 100% accurate impossible. Even the names of some of these westerners remain suspect, with three or four different spellings left behind, an assortment of aliases being used, and in the case of certain criminals, falsified information being given to authorities, for obvious reason, but mistakenly accepted as correct at the time, then passed down as such through the ages.

One thing is certain. The West from the 1850's to the early 1920's was hardly the nice, wholesome place some writers have made it out to be, nor was it the romantic, dashing sharpshooter's haven seen in films. This book offers a closer, truer look at the activities and lives of various personalities, good and bad, famous and not-so-famous, who left some type of mark on history.

It does not claim 100% faultlessness, but has been based on multiple sources and lengthy research, bringing about something more truthful than many previously-published half-myths concerning a West that never existed. If errors are to be found, these rely upon the fault of conflicting information drawn from existing documents and research material. A wealth of reference materials does exist on the West, encouraging any scoffers or doubters to do their own investigation of detail they might find contrary to what they have heard or read before. It is not this author's intention to add to the growing slushpile which has made fact and fiction inseparably bound together.

As for the people of the wild West, what were they really like? The best description might be found in an old advertisement from the Sergio Leone film, "Once Upon A Time In The West." While the movie did nothing to shatter the fairy-tale atmosphere of western times, the following quote sums up the spirit of western life better than any other. It is with this same attitude, this book is being presented to the reader.

"Once upon a time in the West there were men like this. They were not noble; they were not heroic. They simply were."

Dale Pierce

CLAY ALLISON

(1840 - 1887)

Gunfighter

In truth, Robert "Clay" Allison was no romantic hero of the West, but a strange, unpredictable psychopath who drank heavily and enjoyed the company of ladies of the evening, when he wasn't shooting people for illogical reasons.

His antics were varied, ranging from deplorable to perverse, yet somehow these have been forgotten in the novels and history books in favor of the more glamorous, yet entirely untrue image of a fancy-dressed, gun-toting, real-life superman.

If Allison really had any of the quick-draw skills attributed to him, they were seldom made evident. When he killed, it was invariably when the odds were in his favor — an opponent was drunk, or he had the drop on the man he intended to blast away.

In spite of this, he always managed to escape the hangman's noose for murder, relying on a self-defense excuse and possibly bullying which made others afraid to testify against him. He must not have been that great with a gun, though, as one story circulates of his accidentally shooting himself in the foot.

The myth of the galloping gunman is destroyed by existing records showing just how and why Allison killed, proving a bloodlust most modern-day mass-murderers have failed to equal.

Another incident tells of how, in 1870, he fought a duel with knives in New Mexico, when the challenger reportedly felt he'd be outclassed with pistols. That same year, he served as the ringleader in a lynching, after which he cut off the victim's head and gave it to a friend for exhibition in a bar. Again, not exactly what might be filed under the category of normal or heroic behavior.

Strangest of all would not be this gunman's mean streak or his eagerness to kill, but the peculiar habit of liking to get drunk, take off his clothes, ride naked through town, then calmly walk into a saloon and order a drink. Uncanny behavior, to the fullest extent, was something he thrived on.

In the end, fate proved unkind to "Clay" Allison, who was denied the right to die in a gunfight or in some other daredevil way, which would have propelled him toward the same dubious immortality of Wyatt Earp, Billy The Kid, and other pseudo-gunfighters who have been romanticized by the media.

In a highly-intoxicated state, he fell off a wagon and the wheel rolled over him, breaking his neck. The body of this puzzling kill-crazy legend was laid to rest in Pecos, Texas.

BRONCHO BILLY ANDERSON

(1883 - 1971)

Film Star

Born as Max Aronson in Pine Bluff, Arkansas, this one-day star of the silent screen grew up on the outskirts of what was one of the wildest areas in the entire West, living in the shadow of outlaw legends, hangings, and dime-novel myths, which, as an actor, he sought to portray on screen.

While the West that really was must have surely been familiar to him, he and many others devoted their time to exploiting the legends of quick-drawing gunmen, loyal lawmen, and ugly, snarling villians.

Changing his name to Broncho Billy Anderson, which was the incorrect spelling of the Spanish word "bronco," and carried about as such through his career, he became an idol to the matinee set, who failed to realize the rest of his stage name had been derived from one Bloody Billy Anderson, a midwestern plunderer of the worst order.

Anderson started his film career in cooperation with the experiments of Thomas Edison, who was dabbling in movie film at the turn of the century. His first piece was the 1902 release, "The Messenger Boy's Mistake," directed by Ed Porter. This was followed by an all-time classic, "The Great Train Robbery," in which he received a major part, nearly blown when he informed the production staff he did not know how to ride a horse.

His lone attempt to mount the animal proved such a disaster, it was decided for the duration of the film, he would only be seen in the robbery scenes on foot. In spite of being the cowboy who feared horses, he continued active in the film world until 1965, when he made his last film, "The Bounty Killer."

In 1958, he was presented with a special Oscar for his work in the Western genre and died in 1971.

IRA ATEN

(1862 - 1953)
Texas Ranger

One of the final figures of Western lore, Ira Aten lived for decades after the era of gunfighters, bad men, and bandits passed away, providing historians with many details which survive today.

He found his call to fame while only 20, when he joined the Texas Rangers, rising from the rank of private to captain of Company D in the Frontier Battalion.

While carrying on the fight for law and order, he saw additional activity as well, serving as sheriff of Fort Bend County while still active in the Rangers.

Shifting his interests to a more political field, he resigned his captain's position to serve as a lawman in Castro County.

Finally bored with chasing outlaws and, more often than not, petty crooks, he switched trades altogether, becoming manager of the gigantic XIT Ranch, a position he held for a decade. While he handled his duties with the same effectiveness that he'd shown as a lawman, this profession likewise started to bore him.

In the early 1900's he decided to move to California, where he invested in property and other businesses. From that point onward, he lived an uneventful life, barring the tales he told of his days when the West was less refined.

He died in El Centro on August 5, 1953, at the age of 91, an event which in itself would have surprised many of his long-gone Ranger friends, who would most assuredly have expected him to have been killed in some adventure or shootout.

SAM BASS

(1851 - 1878)
Outlaw

Born in Indiana, this drifter showed up in Texas at a young age, where he held down a series of legitimate jobs, prior to becoming a criminal.

Acting as leader of a small gang of crooks, he engineered various robberies, most of them minor until September of 1877, when the band held up a Union Pacific train at Big Springs. This heist netted them over $60,000 in gold coins.

Suddenly finding the law more interested in his capture, Bass ordered his associates to split up, each taking $10,000. He then rode to Denton County, where he met two new associates, Frank Jackson and Henry Underwood. Recruiting them, he set out to form an entirely new gang, figuring it would throw lawmen for a loop. It did!

In 1878, he pulled off a series of train robberies in rapid order, but time was running out as spring drew to a close. The Pinkerton Agency, US marshals, Texas Rangers, sheriffs, and bounty hunters were all looking for the bandit leader.

On July 21st of that year, he rode into Round Rock, intent on robbing the local bank, but someone had informed on him and gunmen were waiting. Shots were fired, with the outlaw managing to kill one of his assailants before making his escape, mortally wounded with a bullet in his back.

The trackers found him later that day, lying on the ground, near death. A short time afterward, he breathed his last.

The bandit was buried at the local graveyard in Round Rock, where his marker may still be seen.

ROY BEAN

(1825? - 1903)
Pseudo-judge / Saloonkeeper

Born in Kentucky, this dumpy, rumpled character emerged in Texas as the self-proclaimed "Law West Of The Pecos," although the type of law he meted out borderlined between brutal and comical.

Unlike Judge Parker at Fort Smith, who had a legal right to do as he did, gaining the reputation of a "hanging judge," Bean sought the same distinction without paying particular attention to what jurisdiction belonged to him. Surprisingly, Texas Rangers and others seemed happy to accept his peculiarities as binding in this land, which was infested with every type of criminal mentionable.

Bean, a fanatical fan of entertainer Lillie Langtry, let his fantasies run wild, establishing a tiny community named in her honor. Likewise, he dubbed the saloon in which he rendered both drinks and justice with equal enthusiasm, "The Jersey Lilly." Although the spelling was incorrect, the thought was in the right place.

Like Judge Parker, who became known for his rages at the bench, Bean's antics were sometimes bizarre. He once fined a lawyer for using profanity in his courtroom, by misunderstanding the words "habeas corpus" as gutter talk, rather than legal jargon.

Obviously knowing little about the law he supposedly represented, his decisions, actions, and words of wisdom reached almost mythological proportions. Bean evidently relished such publicity as well, driving himself to even stranger behavior in order to live up to the legacy circulating about him.

Many speculated his near-maniacal mannerisms were a front designed to attract the attention of Lillie Langtry, as the judge himself became a national celebrity, when the media got wind of his story.

During the last few years of his life, prior to a drawn-out death stemming from alcoholism in 1903, the old man tried intently to provoke a visit from the famed actress/singer.

Langtry did finally come to the town named in her honor, but it was too late. Roy Bean died 10 months beforehand.

FRED BEELL

(18?? - 1925)

Wrestler

Fred Beell *(Photo from the collection of Charles E. Gilbert)*

While charges of fakery abound in today's world of professional wrestling, things were taken much more seriously in the time of Fred Beell, who reportedly could go either way, meaning if circumstances fit his needs, he would be more than willing to fix the end of a bout, but when provoked, could hurt a man faster than he could blink his eyes.

Throughout the southwest and midwest, his name was well recognized, both before and after his reign as World Heavyweight Champion. During a lengthy career, he had many victories over formidable opponents, the most important being Frank Gotch.

In truth, Beell was well on the way to losing this 1906 confrontation, when his opponent accidentally tripped and struck his head on a ringpost, knocking himself out. From there a pin was easy, but the triumph was shortlived. Gotch asked for a rematch, got it, and scored a humiliating win.

Beell died in a car crash in 1925, but one of the holds he introduced to the wrestling world lives on, used interchangeably in "real" action as well as "staged" shows.

The move, called "The Beell Throw" or more simply, "The Beell," involves hooking an opponent by the neck and beneath the shoulder, then hurling him across the ring like a big beach ball. This, once Beell's trademark move, used just before pinning his challengers, was later duplicated by others and incorporated into their matches. Though this hold is seen on nearly every wrestling show broadcast today, its inventor has sadly faded into oblivion.

BILLY THE KID

(1859 - 1881)
Gunfighter

Much has been said about Billy The Kid in print, film, and song, the bulk of it being untrue.

In actuality, the real Billy The Kid was not left-handed. He was not illiterate. He did not kill 21 men, presumedly one for every year he lived, as even his actual age at the time of death has come into dispute. He did not rob from the rich and give to the poor.

His given name was not William Bonney, this being an alias he assumed later down the road, but the unflattering Henry McCarty, which sounds scarcely as menacing. He did not have the quick draw attributed to him, as the majority of his vicitims, a realistic fatality toll ranging between four to ten, were ambushed or shot while unarmed.

He did, however, like to chew tobacco, flirt with the ladies, and even attempt to play the piano. While he never married, there are some indications he might have fathered three or more children with different women.

The Kid did not kill his first man at the age of 12 to avenge his mother's honor, his first victim being one Frank P. Cahill, shot through the stomach during a disputed card game. Though the much larger Cahill had slapped Billy around after charging him with cheating and may have deserved what he received, the law didn't see it that way. The Kid was jailed, only to make an escape and begin the rampage which would later become legendary.

Had it not been for the infamous Lincoln County Range War, Billy The Kid might have faded away, but seeking employment by British rancher John Tunstall dropped him unwittingly into the line of fire. When Tunstall was murdered, The Kid and his friends sought out the killers.

As the body count continued to rise, Billy found himself the hunted rather than the hunter. Murder charges were directed against him and his associates, leading him to flee lawmen, bounty hunters, and avengers from the range wars.

The newspapermen in the East caught wind of his story and quickly turned him into the most high-profile outlaw since Jesse James. While Billy's jailbreaks, shootouts, and escapes from life-threatening situations were to an extent verified, a great deal of what is commonly believed about him today comes not from fact, but the ink of these numerous writers who created Robin Hood-styled adventures for him to make up for the lagging moments where reality moved too slowly.

In truth, the history books do record some dramatic scenes, such as Billy's capture by Pat Garrett when cornered in a cabin, surrendering only after shoving his badly-wounded associate, Charlie Bowdre, out the door to be riddled by bullets, justifying the action by saying, "They've killed you, Charlie, but you can get a few of them before you die."

A highly-publicized trial followed, The Kid being sentenced to hang. From behind bars the condemned man wrote letters to Governor Lew Wallace, asking to see him and hinting the desire to cut some sort of deal. When this failed, he took the more direct approach, escaping from jail and killing two men in the process. Freedom did not last long.

On July 14, 1881, Billy The Kid was shot by Pat Garrett in a darkened room on Pete Maxwell's ranch, where he'd holed up in Fort Sumner. He was buried in the local graveyard, between Tom O'Folliard, a former gang member, and the aforementioned Charlie Bowdre.

RUFUS BUCK

(18?? - 1896)
Outlaw

Rufus Buck, a Ute Indian, was a plunderer who went on a short-term rampage in the summer of 1895, creating a 13-day reign of terror unmatched in brutality and perversion.

Along with a gang of youthful, half-breed associates (Lucky Davis, Lewis Davis, Maomi July, and Sam Sampson), he swarmed across Oklahoma's Cherokee Territory. During their violent spree, the gang shot a black man, killing him for no justifiable reason, stole whatever they could get their hands on, and raped two women. A deputy U.S. Marshal was likewise included among the fatalities, while other holdups followed in short order.

On August 10, their criminal campaign came to an end, when Buck and his gang were captured without a shot being fired, the five hoodlums surrendering to an army of U. S. marshals and Indian police. Taken to Fort Smith for trial, justice was swift in coming. Judge Isaac Parker, shaking with rage at many points during testimony, was more than eager to render the death penalty following a guilty verdict for the entire Buck gang.

On July 1, 1896, Buck and his four accomplices were hanged en masse from a single scaffold. Prior to his death, the bandit leader had evidently found religion or attempted to atone with divinity for his sins.

A poem was found in his cell, written in the design of a cross and marked with several Christian overtones. While the rest of Fort Smith felt certain the marauder was on his way to hell, he thought differently and was confident, through repentance, he'd be going from the gallows to heaven.

Which destination was his after death remains as speculative and questionable as details concerning his life prior to the short-lived rampage.

KIT CARSON

(1809 - 1868)
Mountain Man

Kit Carson *(Photo: New Mexico State Records Center and Archives)*

Born as Christopher Carson, he took the nickname of "Kit" early in life. This man's exploits would make several books in their own right.

Busy in both the Mexican-American War and the Civil War, an active go-between in Indian conflicts, an explorer with uncanny skills for survival, and a smooth talker who might have made an outstanding politician, had he chosen to do so, are all attributes given to this legendary figurehead of Western lore.

Unlike many criminals, confidence men, and psychotics who would come later, only to be immortalized as undeserved heroes after death a la Jesse James, Billy The Kid, and Wyatt Earp, Carson's character carries few historical blemishes. One might honestly say he stands out as a rarity, a person who lives up to the praise directed his way.

While Carson's various lines of work caused him to travel considerably, it was New Mexico that always remained his favorite spot. He died peacefully from a hemorrhage on May 23, 1868, shortly after his wife had passed away from natural causes in April. Both were buried in Taos, in a small cemetery near their old home. Both this homestead and graveyard have been turned into a museum, which still may be visited by tourists.

While sometimes considered an avid Indian fighter, thanks to confusion with his nephew, William, who took the name of Kit Carson to the stage in a circus act, this man was actually sympathetic to the Navajo, Kiowa, and other tribes. In 1864, one of his last great acts was negotiating a peaceful surrender of over 8,000 warring Indians.

WILLIAM CARSON

(1858 - 1957)
Scout / Showman

Born in New Mexico on August 7, 1858, William Carson eventually took on the nickname of Kit, just as his famous Uncle Christopher had done.

He held various jobs during his adult life, including work as a teamster, cowboy on cattle drives, ranch hand and U. S. Cavalry Scout. One of his most glorious accomplishments occurred while under the command of Captain Lawton, in which he helped track and capture Geronimo in the Dragoon Mountains, during the Indian's 1886 rampage. He also took part in the Sioux War, up in the Dakotas.

With the approach of the 1900's, the West was changing. Rather than struggling with the old ways, as did "The Wild Bunch" and others unable to shift with the time, Carson decided to exploit himself, a logical choice of alternatives as opposed to outlawry.

Joining a circus act, he traveled the United States, profiting on the East's fascination with Western lore. The Kit Carson name proved to be a big drawing card, which brought the frontiersman to Europe as well.

In 1930, at the age of 72, he decided to retire from this way of life as well. He headed back for New Mexico, where he still refused to fade away. He engaged in various activities, continued to spin tales, and worked for the Roswell Ration Board during World War II. In 1957, at the incredible age of 99, he finally passed away, alert and intelligent right to the end.

While his stage show greatly altered and shifted his real-life exploits, adding to the fabrication of Wild West lore we still see today, there was more than a moderate segment of fact mingled in as well.

Few other people better demonstrate how easily legend and reality mix together, than in this man, who gained fame while still alive, feeding the fuels of his own story, rather than gaining recognition via films, campfire tales, or bold-faced lies told long after his death.

BUTCH CASSIDY

(1866 - 1909)
Outlaw

Butch Cassidy was actually one of many aliases used by Utah-born Robert Leroy Parker.

Rising from a petty crook to one of the most celebrated train and bank robbers of his era, a curious sidenote is the fact that he never killed a man, in spite of his sinister reputation. While he looked nothing like Paul Newman, who played him in the famous film, Butch Cassidy & The Sundance Kid, he was in real-life just as amiable as the screen adaptation.

Wise-cracking and as easy-going as could be expected for a bandit leader, he was more of a "clown" than "king" of Western outlawry. Stories of his antics abound, as when, after a Nevada bank robbery in which he and his band made a clean escape with a good deal of cash, he sent the bank manager an autographed photo, with a word of thanks. Hardly a gesture becoming a man who supposedly spread terror through not only North, but South America as well.

In the company of "The Wild Bunch" it seemed unlikely Cassidy would have had leadership capacity, but he did, although he was no gunman, unlike Deaf Hanks, Kid Curry, Bill Carver (whom Cassidy often commented smelled like a skunk), Harry Tracy, and a host of others who had no hesitations whatsoever to kill without provocation.

From the early 1890's to the early 1900's, he remained one of the most elusive robbers around, chased by lawmen, Pinkertons, bounty hunters, and railroaders. Realizing the outlaw era was quickly coming to an end in the United States, he, The Sundance Kid, and the girlfriend they both shared, a former schoolteacher named Etta Place, packed up for Argentina via cruise ship. It didn't take them long to make themselves known, in spite of original intentions to live honest lives.

Soon, Cassidy and Sundance were robbing banks throughout Argentina, Peru, and Bolivia, borderlining between heists by working in a tin mine. The pair of bandits greatly underestimated the South Americans and their system of justice, however, with their luck running out in 1909.

Cornered in San Vicente, Bolivia, the outlaws were overwhelmed by troops who had no intentions of taking them alive. Sundance was wounded and either died from his injuries or was shot by Cassidy, before he, too, chose suicide as a final escape.

Did Butch Cassidy really die this way? The odds seem most likely, although gossip spread that Butch and Sundance both escaped South America alive, taking advantage of their "death notices" when in fact, the two men killed in the confrontation with troops had been other, minor outlaws.

American audiences have always been spellbound by stories of impossible capers, switch-offs, and romanticism of this sort, as it's sometimes hard to let legends die. Still, most evidence points to the fact that Cassidy and The Kid both met their end on South American soil.

BILLY CLAIBORNE

(1860? - 1882)
Outlaw

A loudmouthed, troublesome post-teen who used so many derivations of his name, including Clairborne and Clayborn, the correct spelling or even if this was his rightful identity could be disputed.

Among the aliases, he liked being called "Arizona's Billy The Kid" and tried to impress upon others his ability with a pistol. A chance to prove this in a face to face gunfight at the OK Corral was blown in 1881, when this self-proclaimed "Billy The Kid" decided it better to run away, along with Ike Clanton.

He did, however, add at least one notch to his credit when he shot a drunk named Frank Hickey in a Tombstone saloon, putting a bullet in his head at close range. Reasons for this vary, some sources saying the man believed Claiborne to be the "real" Billy The Kid and insisting they drink together, others claiming an unrelated argument or the victim's scoffing at his killer's chosen alias being the reason.

In any case, Claiborne let his ego get the better of him in 1882, when, drunk, he had words with Buckskin Frank Leslie. The latter bounced the former out of the saloon where the confrontation took place. Waiting outside, the pseudo-Billy The Kid planned to avenge this insult via ambush, but Leslie, knowing what was up, turned the tables on him. Badly wounded, Claiborne supposedly blurted out amid choice profanities, "don't shoot! I'm already killed!" His words proved true and he died a short time later in great agony.

His remains were planted in Boot Hill, the same graveyard where his earlier victim, Frank Hickey, was taken. His killer later got in trouble with the law himself, spent time in jail, and vanished after his release.

BILLY CLANTON

(1862 - 1881)
Gunshot Victim

While Billy Clanton grew up within a family of outlaws, his young age leads historians to wonder whether he, too, was involved in the Clanton-McLowery cattle rustling empire or if he was simply a bystander, waiting for a chance to get in the "business end" of things, like his older brothers.

While some have viewed him as a youth caught up in the gunfire of the OK Corral gundown in Tombstone, Arizona, on October 26, 1881, which pitted the rustlers against the Earp brothers and Doc Holliday, this may not have been the real case. He was no angel, by indication of the fury in which he dove into battle, quite possibly being the first man to draw his gun.

Although dressed in overalls and not having come looking for a fight, he proved to have a certain childish bloodlust, managing to wound both Virgil and Morgan Earp, even after being downed with holes in his wrist, chest, and stomach. Reportedly, he was still trying to fire his empty gun from a dying position, asking not to be given medical aid, but more ammunition, as he was disarmed.

He might have been better off, had he duplicated the actions of his older brother, Ike, who after egging on the showdown, turned tail and ran, or lesser-ranking brother, Phineas, who didn't even come into town that day.

As it was, he died shortly after the gunfight ended, no longer masquerading under a veil of bravado, but screaming in agony as he realized the end was near. Morphine was given to calm him somewhat, but his heart gave out before further treatment was administered.

He lies in Tombstone's Boot Hill graveyard to this day.

Note: Historians have identified the name variously as McLaurie, McLaury, McLowery, and McLowry.

IKE CLANTON

(18?? - 1887)

Rancher / Outlaw

History has branded Joseph Isaac Clanton as one of the most detestable men who ever walked the West and while he was by no means an angel of mercy, much of his sinister reputation has been overblown.

Taking over the Clanton Ranch after his father's death and thus inheriting the criminal empire left behind, he quickly expanded illegal activities of all forms, especially the rustling of cattle. While an antagonistic, bragging, chest-thumping coward who lacked the capability to back up the threats he made on his own, he was also somewhat of a criminal genius, an amazing fact considering his limited education.

Constantly, he showed cunning and craftiness in his long-lasting grudge with the Earps, John Clum, Doc Holliday and others, via bribery, influencing corrupt lawmen, hiring a host of outlaws to do his dirty work for him, and after the OK Corral, engineering plots to kill the surviving participants.

As for the OK Corral gun battle, history again points to Ike as the troublemaker who started it all, then ran, deserting his friends when the firing started. Behind the scenes, however, he may not have been the total villain and at one point long before, may have even been an under-the-table business partner with the Earps.

Some time before the shootout, a stagecoach had been robbed. The Earps and Holliday blamed the Clanton mob. The Clantons, in turn, blamed the Earps. Some speculation exists that both parties may have been involved, with bad feelings or a doublecross stemming from this, which fanned the flames toward all-out war.

A closer look at the Earps, particularly Wyatt, reveals a less-than-honorable picture. Mainly due to Wyatt's version of what happened and accounts from the *The Tombstone Epitaph,* a "pro-Earp" paper, the Clantons have been painted as completely black, which they were not, while the Earp brothers were anything but holy white vestals of purity.

Following the OK Corral incident, which proved a great fiasco for the rustlers, Ike set about gaining revenge from a distance. In the same manner Al Capone would use decades later in gangster-ruled Chicago, the bandit leader designed slick ambushes which left Morgan Earp dead, Virgil Earp crippled, and Wyatt far more worried about his life than he ever admitted. Getting some friends of his own together, he retaliated to the Clanton backlash, forcing Ike to leave for Mexico on a "business trip" that kept him out of Arizona until his old enemy left.

As the 1880's drew to a close, Ike made an attempt to rebuild his fallen empire with the aid of his mysterious brother, Phineas, and failed miserably. Most of his associates, such as John Ringo, Florentino Cruz, Pete Spence, Johnny Behan, Frank Stillwell, Curly Bill, Pony Deal, Wes Fuller, Billy Claiborne, and Frank McLowery were either gone or dead. Hard times had arrived.

In 1887, Commodore Perry Owens became the new sheriff in Apache County, indicating the day of the badman was over. He kept good his promise by catching the remaining Clanton brothers on a rustling charge. Phineas decided to give up, but Ike, finally showing the courage to draw a gun, tried to shoot his way to freedom.

It was the wrong move to make and he was shot dead, his actual ticket to the graveyard being punched in a manner far different than various Hollywood movies, where he always seems to die by Wyatt Earp's hand.

OLD MAN CLANTON

(18?? - 1881)

Outlaw

Originating from Texas, he was legally known as N. H. Clanton, which some historians claim stood for Newman Hayes or Newman Haines, but this remains speculative as he readily accepted being called "Old Man" by friend and foe alike.

After relocating in Arizona, near present-day Tombstone, he set up a virtual empire based on rustling and other activities. With the aid of his misfit sons, he saw his profits grow, but his dream of becoming the all-time king of criminal enterprise was cut short via an ambush.

Having led the slaughter of 19 Mexicans in order to steal a mule train and make off with an estimated $75,000 in silver bullion, his guilt was not proven, but suspicion was strong enough to call for retaliation from the opposite side of the border. A few weeks after this robbery, he returned to Mexico for a cattle drive, the only problem being the stock he was herding toward his Arizona homebase belonged to someone else. He was followed by a band of angry Mexicans, who shot him and the rest of his crew, leaving only one survivor behind.

Old Man Clanton's grave may be seen in Tombstone's Boot Hill. His infamous Clanton Ranch also stands outside that city, existing in ruin except for a sign and some adobe walls. Efforts were once considered to restore it, but were abandoned, although local people still direct a tourist from time to time, to the crumbling spread. An unpaved road and difficult hike make visiting for most people a difficult chore.

What was once the central office for this old outlaw's projected criminal kingdom, died away, just like his empire.

PHINEAS CLANTON

(Birth & death unknown)

Outlaw

Phineas Clanton, otherwise known as "Finn" by his associates, was a shadowy figure in the high-profile outlaw family.

He did not partake in his father's robberies or ranch raids into Mexico. He was nowhere to be seen during the gunfight at the OK Corral. Little exists in the history books concerning his activities, while most films such as "Gunfight At The OK Corral," "Hour Of The Gun," "Doc," don't even admit to his existence, aiming their attention on his more verbose brother, Ike, instead.

Visitors to Tombstone and even a good number of residents would have no knowledge of him or his activities, most likely figuring "Finn Clanton" to be the product of some novelist's imagination. He did exist, however, even if he managed to escape or to be denied the infamy accredited to the rest of the clan.

Some speculation exists that Phineas may have finally gotten involved in the family feud following the death of brother Billy, quite possibly taking part in the shooting of Morgan Earp. In 1887, he and Ike took to rustling cattle in Apache County. Trailed by lawmen to their base camp on the Blue River, "Finn" showed his true colors by surrendering on the spot. He received a long jail sentence for his trouble, while Ike decided to fight it out and was gunned down.

Little else remains concerning him after his time spent in prison. Presumedly, he was the only brother of the Clanton gang not to die by gunfire. Attempts by writers, students, and researchers to dig up further information concerning his life have proven frustrating.

JOHN CLUM

(1851 - 1932)
Indian Agent / Pioneer / Journalist

Born in New York, John Clum migrated to New Mexico in 1871, then moved to Arizona in 1874, where he took on duties as an Indian agent.

Overseeing the Apaches at San Carlos, he came to be regarded as one of the most effective officials to ever work among the Indians.

Eventually deciding to improve himself, he took to studying law, shrugged off the idea of becoming an attorney, and bought a newspaper business in Tucson, which he sold in 1880. He then put out the paper for which history still holds him best known, *The Tombstone Epitaph*.

While writing for, editing, and publishing this tabloid, he was a high-profile Tombstonian, noted for his hard-line backing of the Earps against the Clanton Gang. He was also active in many civic and social activities concerning this fast-paced mining town.

In 1886, Clum packed up and moved again, working briefly for *The San Francisco Examiner* before joining the U. S. Postal Service and skipping around various parts of the country. In 1909, he finally called it quits and retired, settling down to a less-tiring lifestyle. He died in Los Angeles in 1932.

Curiously, Clum never decided to go into politics, which surprised many, for he was an outstanding organizer and motivator, a relatively honest man, an idealist, and had a way with words few could match.

This, however, was not his calling, although a decision to run for public office could have changed his destiny and, in his long lifetime, he was afforded many chances. His only political highspot was a brief stint as mayor of Tombstone. Had he chosen to do so, he might have made it as far as governor.

CROYDEN COOLEY

(18?? - 1917)
Indian Scout / Rancher

While an unglamorous figure by most standards, Croyden Cooley remains an interesting figure in Arizona lore via his founding of the town of Show Low and the strange way the land on which it now stands was acquired.

Settling in the northern portion of what was then Arizona Territory in 1870, Cooley and his partner, Marion Clark, fenced off some 100,000 acres of ranchland to form a mutual business. In time though, their partnership turned sour and they decided to settle ownership of the vast spread through gambling, the winner of a game of Seven Up buying out the other.

Apparently, the game lasted an entire night, with Cooley needing just one point to win. At that moment, Clark proclaimed to his former partner, "You show low and you win!" Cooley cut the deck, produced a deuce of clubs, and claimed victory. The townsite which was soon to follow was promptly named Show Low, in respect to the winning hand.

Barring brief dramatics such as the above, little else of note remains concerning this man, who grew more reclusive as his health started to fail. Historians from the Chamber of Commerce in Show Low state he died on the Apache Reservation on March 18, 1917, from natural causes. Presumedly, he was buried near his homestead on this reservation, but the location of the same is not known. The ranch, unlike the town he named, no longer exists.

Accounts of whatever became of his disgruntled partner likewise vary, as do reasons for the breakup which led to their now famous gambling session.

Scout, rancher, businessman, and above all, lucky gambler, Cooley was neither an outlaw nor a gunfighter, which has caused him to take a back seat to others from these categories, who made names for themselves during the area's more bloody times.

JIM CORBETT

(1866 - 1933)

Boxer

"Gentleman Jim" Corbett *(Photo courtesy Lew Eskin)*

Originally learning his fighting skills by manhandling bullies while still a kid at the St. Ignatius School in San Francisco, Jim Corbett eventually rose in the professional boxing ranks under the gimmick of "Gentleman Jim" as a direct contrast to the hard-brawling, hard-living antics of the widely known John L. Sullivan.

Fighting mainly in the West, he built a massive fan following for himself, although old-timers seemed to deplore the use of gloves over the bare-knuckled brawls of times past.

On September 7, 1892, Corbett defeated the legendary Sullivan in New Orleans to be declared World Heavyweight Champion. His reign continued until 1897, when he lost a controversial match to Bob Fitzsimmons in Nevada and with it the coveted championship crown.

He continued to fight long afterward, without ever regaining his lost throne. His last contest, incredibly, was a 1928 exhibition against Gene Tunney, at a Manhattan theatre.

Corbett remained a colorful individual throughout his long career and, whenever in the public eye, was careful not to let his "Gentleman" image down. Whenever attending social functions, he would wear the same fancy suits and hats which were used for his publicity photographs, when not in boxing gear.

He died at Bayside, Long Island, on February 18, 1933, after a short illness. With his death, so passed one of boxing's most charismatic eras, a possible forerunner to the hype and glitter of today's gimmick-riddled bouts.

GEORGE CROOK

(1828 - 1890)
Military

After the Civil War, George Crook took to Indian fighting, and was sent to Arizona in 1871 upon the special request of President Grant as a solution to the growing conflicts in the area.

Four years later, he was sent to deal with Sioux uprisings. In 1882, he was once again called to Arizona, where renegades were leaving the Apache Reservation. Crook again quelled the bulk of the conflicts, with the help of other military leaders, chasing down, among others, the infamous Geronimo.

One of the reasons why the General's campaigns were so effective, ironically enough, was due to his reliance on Indian scouts and trackers, a policy some of his compatriots evidently thought absurd. In 1886, with the Apache holdouts surrendering, it became an injustice to many of these scouts, who had worked loyally for the United States, to be deported to Florida along with the warriors they'd hunted down.

Crook campaigned vocally against what had been done, leading to a split with many former friends, including a past cohort, General Miles. Strangely, the once-dreaded Indian fighter became a champion for the red man's cause, working constantly to better living conditions for both the Apache and the Sioux.

General Crook died in March of 1890. After his passing, Indian and Anglo relationships continued to drag downward. The Indians, too, seemed to realize they had lost more than an enemy. They had lost a spokesman.

FLORENTINO CRUZ

(18?? - 1882)
Outlaw

This shifty character showed up in Tombstone, Arizona, where he was hired on by the Clantons.

Although he spoke of himself as a fast-handed gunman, he was considered a blowhard by most of his associates. For a long while, he was given actual ranching duties, without being allowed to take part in the rustling, as he wasn't trusted or thought of as capable enough to follow instructions.

In spite of this, he did supposedly take part in the killing of Morgan Earp, which put vindictive brother Wyatt hot on his trail, along with a small band of friends.

While hiding out on the range, Cruz was found dead with several bullet holes in his body. Two versions exist as to what happened, one told by Wyatt Earp, who claimed to confront the half-breed in an open duel.

The stipulation was that Doc Holliday would count to three. Earp would wait to the final number and still beat his opponent, who would be allowed to go for his gun any time he chose. Under these conditions, if true, Cruz proved himself no gunfighter, in spite of his claims to be otherwise, and was still second-best in the showdown.

The more probable version of what happened contended that Earp and Holliday found their prey asleep and filled him full of lead without even bothering to wake him.

In either case, the petty outlaw was just as dead and was taken to Tombstone's Boot Hill, where his grave may still be seen. On the marker, he is listed only as Florentino, with no last name tagged on.

KID CURRY

(1870 - 1904)
Gunfighter / Train Robber / Outlaw

Born Harvey Logan in Dodson, Missouri, this outlaw and "Wild Bunch" rider's career of crime stretched from Clinton, Arizona to Knoxville, Tennessee, although he liked to operate out of the midwest.

Sadly, a teenage brother named Lonnie chose to follow him in a life of crime, only to die in a shootout with lawmen in 1900, while trying to live up to the reputation of being Kid Curry's kinsman.

As is the case with most bandits, robbers, and gunmen, Kid Curry's exploits were greatly distorted and added to, although during his career, he remained an undeniably mean piece of work. Eight men at least, maybe more, were verified victims of his guns, including three sheriffs.

His unbelievable jailbreaks, reckless train holdups, and willingness to fight left him branded as a dangerous psychopath who drank heavily and couldn't care less whether he lived or died, yet this same man remained suave with the ladies, wooing several girlfriends when he found the time. Well-groomed, well-dressed, and articulate, he seemed anything but the kill-crazy madman lingering beneath the surface.

On June 7, 1904, he pulled his last robbery, holding up the Denver & Rio Grande at Parachute, Colorado, not anticipating the tracking party that dogged him to Glenwood Springs, where in order to avoid capture, he took the option of shooting himself.

As with Butch Cassidy, The Sundance Kid, and other "Wild Bunch" riders, he made the fatal mistake of failing to see the Wild West he once knew coming to a close. The days of the glamorous bandits, worshipped like heroes by an adoring public were fast ending, with law and order starting to prevail.

For "The Wild Bunch," it was change or die and Kid Curry, like his compatriots, chose the latter.

PAULINE CUSHMAN

(1833 - 1893)
Entertainer / Spy

Born in New Orleans, Pauline left home at a young age, taking to a theatrical career as an actress and singer, all the while furiously protecting her dignity, meaning unlike many counterparts, she did not use the stage as a front for prostitution.

During the Civil War, however, she was not above using her career as a mask for work as a Union spy, extracting secrets from the high-ranking Confederate officers who patronized her shows. Eventually caught, she was destined for execution, but she was rescued by friends and rushed to safety behind Northern lines.

Afterward, her career took a nosedive, rather than climbing, and she settled in Casa Grande, Arizona, to an ill-fated marriage. Cushman left her husband, announced plans for a theatrical comeback, and headed for California, where once again, promised deals went sour.

From that point onward, she was forced to take demeaning jobs such as scrubbing floors and cleaning to keep from starving. At the time of her death, she was living in San Francisco and nearly broke. The Grand Army of the Republic paid for her burial and, later, a historical notation about her work as a spy for the Union against the Confederates, was affixed to her marker.

During her long and roller-coaster stage career, she portrayed a tranquil, easy-going woman, but away from public eye she was nothing of the kind, flying into blind rages when propositioned by steamed-up male fans. More than once, she attacked a would-be Romeo with anything she could get her hands on, including on one occasion, a horse whip.

GEORGE DAVES

(1867 - 1888)
Miner / Romantic

The story of George Daves reads like the script for a soap opera.

Growing up in Tombstone, Arizona, he was infatuated by a local teenage beauty named Cleopatra Edmunds, but whatever advances he made toward her were quickly turned down. Acting on impulse, this would-be Western Romeo figured he could gain his love's attention with money and went off to work in a mine outside Casa Gande. When he returned, he immediately set out to score a triumph.

Somehow, he managed to talk the girl into accompanying him to a social function, where his advances again were shrugged off and he was left alone. Cleopatra decided to let someone else escort her home. At this point his mind must have snapped, for he spent a sleepless night, then plotted to take revenge.

The following afternoon, Daves took a gun and walked to the girl's house. She saw him coming and took off running, but he pursued, firing all the while. Two bullets hit the girl, and thinking his mission complete, the young man saved the final shot for himself, putting a bullet in his brain.

The tragedy did not end in the dramatic murder-suicide Daves intended. Although he, himself, was killed on the spot by the well-placed bullet fired through his head, his aim was otherwise faulty.

Cleopatra suffered two injuries, one in the arm, the other in the lung, but since no accounts of her death are found, must have recovered from the onslaught, going on to live as normal a life as possible under the circumstances.

PONY DEAL

(18?? - 1882)
Outlaw

Like many of the drifters who came to Arizona to work as cowboys or prospectors, little remains on record about this mysterious gunman, presumedly a half-breed, who took up quarters at the Clanton Ranch.

While he showed readiness to break the law if it meant a profit, he was always missing when gunplay came into effect, such as at the OK Corral. While he may have been in on the shooting attacks on the two Earp brothers or at least been made aware of the game plan, nothing of this order has ever been proven. It's not unlikely to think the bulk of his work on the Clanton spread was carrying out the functions of a legitimate handyman, kept as a gun in reserve, and used on rustling activities.

Things got hot for Deal in January of 1882 when he took part in the robbery of a Tombstone-Bisbee stage. Later that year, he reputedly killed a gambler known as O'Rourke, who some insisted was wanted for murder himself under the alias of Johnny-Behind-The-Deuce. Deal decided it best to head for other places, time closing in on the Arizona outlaw bands.

He started hanging around the Arizona-New Mexico border, but before 1883 could roll in, he too, was dead, the victim of a shootout.

DENNIS DILDA

(1860's? - 1886)

Outlaw

Dennis Dilda and family *(Photo: Sharlot Hall Museum Library and Archives)*

On the surface Dennis Dilda seemed to be a good husband and father, all the while engaging in petty theft by night.

After his arrival in Prescott, Arizona from Texas, many small crimes were pulled off, including the theft of ducks, turkeys, chickens, and cattle. A series of burglaries also devastated the area, in which food, rather than money, seemed to be a main objective.

Suspicion gradually fell upon the Texan and a lawman named John Murphy was sent to investigate. Dilda, seeing trouble coming, ambushed this man from long range, shot him, and concealed the body in an oat sack, which he buried on his farm.

This crime naturally provoked more suspicion than any small-time larceny and he decided to flee, leaving his wife behind to take the rap for him. This backfired though, for when the woman was put in jail, she told everything.

Dilda was captured and arrested at Ash Fork, near present-day Kingman, after a massive hunting party was formed by Sheriffs Rosenburg and Mulvernon. The killer was returned to Prescott and hanged in February of 1886, on gallows constructed at Willow & West Gurley Streets.

Buckey O'Neill and other celebrated gunmen guarded the prisoner and the scaffold scene, but when the execution took place, many grew ill at ease. O'Neill, in fact, disproved his reputation as a hardcase, growing pale when he saw Dilda riding to the spot where fate awaited him, seated atop his casket in a wagon. When the criminal took the drop, the plucky gunman grew even sicker, and passed out.

BILL DOOLIN

(1863 - 1896)
Outlaw

This Arkansas-born roughneck rode with the Daltons before forming a gang of his own. By the mid-1890's, he had a price on his head of $5,000 dead or alive, thanks to widespread criminal activities. He tried to change in 1894, when he married a minister's daughter. The bearded gunman attempted to go straight, with few triumphant results.

Arrested by a U.S. marshal, while lounging in a public bath, he was transported to Guthrie, Oklahoma to stand trial, but escaped, fleeing to safety in New Mexico. Soon, however, he rejoined his wife, settling in Lawton, Oklahoma, and making a valid attempt to escape his outlaw past.

Enter U.S. Marshal Heck Thomas, who came to the Doolin home and blasted the bandit with his shotgun, killing him on the spot. End of the story? Not hardly, as the truth later revealed.

Thomas, indeed, went to the Doolin cabin, to find the outlaw dead from consumption, his law-abiding widow crying over his demise. Knowing he could not collect a reward on a man found dead from natural causes, the lawman entered the bedroom, blasted the corpse full of buckshot, took it in, claimed he killed the man in a gunfight, and took the $5,000 bounty.

A cunning and dishonest action? Again, not hardly, for Thomas did not pocket the money himself, giving it instead to Doolin's near-penniless widow, so she could start her life afresh.

As for Doolin, he himself possessed a bit more nobility than most of his kind. He once kicked a member out of his gang, when the man shot an unarmed preacher in order to steal his horse.

MORGAN EARP

(1851 - 1882)
Lawman

With his brothers Wyatt, Virgil, and Warren, Morgan Earp has been consistently and perhaps inaccurately played as a great crusader for justice in the wild Southwest.

In truth, how much actual difference existed between any of the Earp clan and the bad men they alledgedly fought would be suspect. Starting his career as a deputy town marshal in Kansas, he later moved to Butte, Montana where, as marshal, he caused a scandal after killing a drunkard named Billy Brooks.

Heading for Arizona, he took a job as a shotgun rider, a position which ended when he assisted his brothers in the celebrated OK Corral gunfight, thanks to a serious bullet wound given by the dying Billy Clanton. The actual gun battle lasted only 30 seconds, with the largest percentage of stories stemming from the incident belonging to myth rather than reality.

With the McLowery brothers and young Clanton dead, a full-scale war was to start. Morgan became one of the fatal retaliations.

On March 17, 1882, as he played pool in Bob Hatch's billiard parlor on Allen Street, he was ambushed in a storm of gunfire, which struck him from behind and hurled him across the room like a gigantic bird. He died a short time later. Brother Wyatt lived to hunt down several presumed participants in the slaughter, without conclusive proof of their guilt.

Thus was born the Earp legacy on which several books and films, most notably "Hour Of The Gun," which depicts Morgan's death in fairly close detail and still crops up infrequently on late-night tv.

VIRGIL EARP

(1843 - 1906)

Lawman

After the Civil War, Virgil Earp began a career in law enforcement as a deputy town marshal in Dodge City, Kansas, before moving to Arizona.

There he invested in a silver mine, while taking up residence in Prescott. He later resettled in Tombstone, where he became a temporary town marshal by appointment, after the death of the original officer, Fred White.

That same year, bad blood between the Earps and the Clanton-McLowery ranchers led to the shootout at the OK Corral. In this gunfight, Virgil received a serious injury, but managed to survive. On December 28, 1881, barely recovered from his wound, he was targeted for death once more as he walked down Allen Street.

The assailants, never truly identified but strongly suspected as Clanton Ranch employees, fired at their intended victim several times, but once again failed to kill him. They did, however, do a fair amount of damage, leaving him a partial cripple for life. Deciding he'd worn out his welcome in Arizona, he moved onward.

In 1887, he was elected marshal of Colton, California, building a saloon in the meantime to become a triumphant businessman. Still not content, he continued to move about, finally dying from pneumonia in Goldfield, Nevada, some time in 1906.

As with his brothers, myth and legend has whitewashed Virgil Earp. In reality, he was suspected of various dishonest dealings pertaining to gambling hall interests throughout his life and was not as well-liked by those around him, as stories claim.

He was no knight in white armor, but no black-cloaked villain either, coming out like most human beings, as a shade of grey.

WARREN EARP

(1855 - 1900)
Lawman

Like Phineas in the Clanton family, Warren might well be considered the forgotten or overlooked member of the Earps, although he, too, dabbled in law enforcement.

Born in Pella, Iowa, he spent most of his early life in California, prior to arriving in Arizona, bent on helping his brothers. The OK Corral gunfight was over, but trouble was brewing on the horizon. Although by no means a gunfighter, he evidently wanted in on the action. He didn't have to wait long.

Serving as a deputy U.S. marshal after Morgan Earp was killed in ambush, Warren joined Wyatt, Doc Holliday and others in the hunting party designed to track down the murderers. How big a role he played in any of the searching or subsequent killing would be questionable.

If Wyatt's version is believable, which it truly isn't, as his reputation for being a liar was well-founded, he gave himself personal credit for shooting down all the criminals in fair fights, without the help of his younger brother or any others.

Still, feeling political heat, Warren decided to leave Arizona in 1882 and did not return until 1900. He took a job as a private detective for the Cattlemen's Association, but did not live long enough to make a name for himself in this function. Shortly after assuming this role, he was shot and killed unimpressively by a drifter named Johnny Boyett, quickly disproving the connections of being a "fast gun" that went with his family name.

Living without much ceremony and dying the same way, he faded into the pages of time without much hoopla, while the rest of his kinsmen became legendary.

WYATT EARP

(1848 - 1929)

Lawman

Wyatt Earp *(Photo:
Sharlot Hall Museum
Library and Archives)*

Perhaps the most laughable character to ever come out of Western lore, Wyatt Earp was little more than an outlaw himself. Films and books, including his own far-fetched autobiography, have made him into a virtuous, gun-toting crusader for morality against everything evil under the sun.

While upholding the law in various places throughout his life, he had no bones about breaking it when it was to his advantage or when a quick profit was there to be had. Some of his shadier doings include crooked gambling interests, running various confidence games, and, of all things, pimping.

Although he claimed to have killed both John Ringo and Bill Brocius, two of his arch-enemies, these boasts prove little more than fantasy. Ringo, found dead against a tree outside Tombstone, Arizona, was killed by an unidentified party while Earp was supposed to have been in Colorado.

While Brocius has often been credited with "dying" at Earp's hand, shot so close by a shotgun that hardly anything remained of the body to be identified, other historians contend this presumed victim left Arizona for Texas, then drifted back through Tombstone in the early 1890's, making his presence known to a few friends, who laughed at his assumed death at the point of Earp's gun, considering it typical of this chest-thumping blowhard.

While Earp's morality certainly stands in question, his courage also becomes evident under fire, as in the OK Corral, when the gunfire started. Rather than run as Ike Clanton and Billy Claiborne did, he stood his ground, facing his assailants and shooting it out with them. Rather than killing his targets in ambush or under other circumstances where the odds were convincingly stacked in his favor, he demonstrated his willingness to go toe-to-toe with his enemies.

After his two brothers were shot by hidden pistoleros,

however, he became less particular about giving others a fair chance to defend themselves. The way in which he tracked down those he suspected of taking part in the assaults against his kinsmen were so frowned upon, he was forced to flee from Arizona.

Earp's saga continued long after the Wild West grew calm. He had his ups and downs, ranging from an arrest for vagrancy to a position of technical advisor for Hollywood films. Other activities included bodyguard, prospector, saloon owner, and, once again, confidence man.

His reputation for fairness and honesty, now readily accepted as a complete fabrication, proved false twice more, once when he was arrested on a fraud charge, and again when accusations were leveled, unproven but generally believed, that as a referee, he fixed the Fitzsimmons-Sharkey boxing match, in order to assist his own gambling interests.

He died in California on January 13, 1929 and although Tombstone requested the cremated ashes for burial in Boot Hill, he was put to rest at the Hills of Eternity Memorial Park in Colma.

On the night of July 6, 1957, the late lawman/crook became a victim of bandits posthumously, when parties unknown stole the 500 pound headstone from the grave plot.

Wyatt Earp, as portrayed by James Garner *(left)* and Henry Fonda *(right)*. *(Photos: Hollywood Book and Poster Shop)*

JOHN EVANS
(1814 - 1897)
Doctor / Politician

Born in Ohio, John Evans was educted in Quaker-backed schools, then obtained a medical degree from Cincinnati College in 1838.

Practicing his trade in Indiana and Illinois, as well as his native Ohio, he contributed much to the medical trade. Included in his actions were the formation of the Indiana Hospital for the Insane and the *Northwestern Medical & Surgical Journal*, a newspaper he created while teaching at Ruth Medical College.

Business also interested him, particularly the investment in real estate, and after converting to the Methodist doctrine, religion became a priority as well. Using the fortune he made off his various land investments, he helped establish Garrett Biblical Institute and Northwestern University.

Naturally, his numerous activities made him a high-profile figure and he decided to enter politics, but did not have the clout he first imagined. Abraham Lincoln came to his aid, appointing him the second territorial governor of Colorado.

Heading west, he took office in 1862, where his accomplishments were far less noteworthy than in the medical field. Scandals followed, with the new governor catching the blame for increasing Indian problems, including a poorly-handled job related to a massive slaughter of reputedly peaceful Indians.

Discredited, perhaps a little unfairly, by his political enemies, the doctor-turned-statesman resigned from office in 1865. Though his political career had hit the rocks, he continued to live in Denver, where he became instrumental in civil affairs, education, social activities, and business ventures.

Most notably, Evans took action when he learned the upcoming transcontinental railroad would by-pass Denver, organizing the creation of the Denver Pacific Railroad to link up with the Union Pacific in Wyoming, thus giving his city a desired link by train, with the rest of the expanding U.S.A.

KING FISHER

(1854 - 1884)

Lawman / Outlaw / Rancher

Following several brushes with the law as a petty crook, John King Fisher, who would later drop the John from his name, grew powerful when he formed a ranch outside of present day Eagle Pass, Texas.

Here he established a clever rustling trade, exchanging stolen American cattle with associates across the border in Mexico, who supplied him with stolen Latin American stock. As his fortune grew, so did his ego, and his tactics to gain attention bordered on the outlandish.

His wardrobe included such uncanny garb as a pair of tigerskin chaps, taken not on a safari, but rather following a raid on a circus group, wide-brimmed sombreros, and gunfighter garb topped off with spangles. "This is King Fisher's Road. Take The Other," was an unfriendly sign adorning the front of his ranch and summed up his disposition fairly well.

Working for and against the law at various intervals, making enemies throughout Texas, and offending many with his arrogance, it's a wonder he died by bullets intended for someone else.

Befriending equally flamboyant criminal/lawman Ben Thompson, he made the mistake of visiting San Antonio, intent on a wild drinking spree. Thompson, however, had more enemies than Fisher, these enemies confronting him and blasting him full of holes. Caught up in the crossfire, Fisher was shot 13 times himself, dying along with his compatriot at the Vaudeville Variety Theatre.

The body, or more accurately what remained of it, was returned to the Fisher ranch for burial.

BOB FITZSIMMONS

(1862 - 1917)
Boxer

This British-born slugger who migrated to the U.S.A. and made a name for himself by the use of his fists, became as much a part of Western lore as many of the lawmen, gunfighters, and outlaws of the time, in fact rubbing elbows with many of them.

In 1896, Fitzsimmons took part in a controversial fight promoted by the wily Judge Roy Bean and an associate named Dan Stuart. While boxing was legally banned in Texas at that time, the two conniving promoters staged the fight on a small island in the center of the Rio Grande river, between America and Mexico.

While angry Texas Rangers stood on a hill far away, lacking the jurisdiction to prevent the fight, Bean racked up a profit, more from selling overpriced beer from his bar/courthouse than in ticket sales. In this controversial match, Fitzsimmons flattened Peter Maher in less than two minutes into the opening round. The winner took home a purse of $8,000, plus an under-the-table $1,000 made on a side bet.

Controversy continued to follow the boxer throughout his career, particularly after his beating Gentleman Jim Corbett for the World Heavyweight Championship on March 17, 1897, in Carson City, Nevada. While Fitzsimmons claimed to gain a victory via a body punch, critics charged it was an illegal, low blow that garnered him the title.

The new champion further angered his enemies and the ex-champ by announcing retirement, a decision which was short-lived. In his first title defense, he was nearly beaten by Jim Corbett, but managed to fight back savagely for a win. He then faced James Jeffries and lost the crown in 1899.

Although he never regained the World Championship, this unusual boxer continued to box well into the turn of the century, although his abilities started to falter. In 1902, he was again beaten by James Jeffries, but refused to hang up the gloves.

He boxed his last match in January of 1914, going to a "no decision" draw with "KO" Sweeny in Williamsport, Pennsylvania. Fitzsimmons was 52 years old at the time.

Bob Fitzsimmons *(Photo courtesy Lew Eskin)*

WILLIAM FLAKE

(1839 - 1932)
Cattle Baron / Land Baron

Born in North Carolina, Flake was taken west by his Mormon parents in 1849, first to Utah, then California, where his father was killed by Indians.

In 1857 he returned to Utah, where he married and took to a life of cattle ranching. By 1877, however, he was dreaming of a better life and headed for Arizona in a wagontrain with other Mormons.

The trip was evidently a rough one, as winter left them stranded, forcing them to cut up canvas for clothing and ration food to stay alive. Finally reaching thier planned destination, Flake again set up a homestead, living the life of a rancher and farmer, growing corn.

It was then that a fellow Mormon, Erastus Snow, came to visit and, unwittingly, history was made. Deciding the homestead was a fine place to start a new Mormon settlement, the two men formed a partnership and went about establishing a town. This town, which still exists, was named Snowflake, not having anything to do with snowfall or the lack of it, as those unfamiliar with the history behind it believe, but as a combination, creatively-designed, moulding of their two last names.

Following the near-fatal attempt to reach Arizona, Flake settled down to a relatively tranquil life, maintaining his labor as farmer and rancher, even as the Mormon colony sprang up about him.

He died from natural causes in 1932, supposedly as sound of wit and memory as any man in his 90's could possibly expect.

PAT GARRETT

(1850 - 1908)

Lawman / Rancher

Born in Alabama, it was not until he came Southwest that this tall, cigar-smoking character began to make a name for himself.

While he held high hopes of a political career which he believed would be enhanced by bringing in Billy The Kid, these aspirations were demolished by the very actions he presumed would stem it along. Rather than receiving him as a conquering hero, the public turned indignant by the way the youthful outlaw had been gunned down in ambush, rather than a drawn-out gunfight on some sunlit street.

Pat Garrett *(Photo: New Mexico State Records Center and Archives)*

Seeing his career as a senator or governor ruined, he sought to write a book on his exploits and gain riches this way, but again, the venture failed. Other lines of work followed, while he devoted time to his wife and family (including a blind daughter who would later become a close associate of the legendary Helen Keller).

Evidently he did not age well, becoming debt-riddled, irritable, and a paranoid. Like Billy The Kid, he was doomed to die in an unglamorous way, contrary to his lifestyle.

On February 29, 1908, following an angry ranch dispute, he was shot through the back of the head while on the open range, as he paused to urinate. Various culprits have since been accused of the killing, including Wayne Brazel, who stood trial but was acquitted, rancher W. W. Cox, and notorious assassin-for-hire, Jim Miller. Originally buried in the old Odd Fellows graveyard in Las Cruces, New Mexico, Pat Garrett's remains were transported to the nearby Masonic Cemetery in 1957.

Unlike the grave of his most famous victim, Billy The Kid, which swarms with tourists visits each year, no one bothers the family plot which carries only "GARRETT" as a tell-tale sign of who lies there.

SUSA GATES

(1856 - 1933)

Educator / Author

A daughter of Mormon pioneer Brigham Young, Susa was born in Salt Lake City, Utah, educated in her father's private school, and attended the University Of Deseret, now known as the University Of Utah.

She studied such things as creative writing, stenography, and, of course, religion. She took to the pen, becoming the first woman to write a novel concerning Mormon life, culture, and belief. She then became founder, publisher, and editor for the *Young Woman's Journal*, remaining active with this from 1889 to 1929, an incredible period of 40 years.

In 1878, she went to the Brigham Young Academy, now known as Brigham Young University, where she taught in the music department. There she met Jacob Gates, whom she married in 1880. In 1897, she organized the domestic science department at this same school, teaching in this area as well as music and theology.

In the midst of this all, she managed to have 13 children, continue numerous writing activities, and become an advocate of suffrage for females, working with the National Council of Women to obtain the right to vote.

From 1914 to the point of her death in 1933, she engaged in yet another editorship, working with the newly founded *Relief Society Magazine*, which branched off from the Relief Society of the Mormon Church.

She also cranked out an abundant stream of biographical works, pieces of fiction, and articles for numerous magazines.

GERONIMO

(1829 - 1909)
Indian leader

While more myth than fact surrounds the life of this Apache warrior, accounts indicate he was never an official chief, but rather a high-ranking medicine man.

Marked as a savage renegade, he and his band of followers were the last holdouts to formally surrender to the U.S. military. His real name, in fact, was Goyakla, meaning "one who yawns" in his native tongue. Geronimo was his adopted name, stemming from the Spanish to English translation of "Jerome" or "Jeromy," for whatever reason. Regardless of which name or alias is chosen to represent him, he remains to this day, the most well-known Indian warrior in history.

Constantly making his escape from the Indian reservations in Arizona, this stocky little man led troops in circles, evaded the most elaborate attempts to contain him, and survived by sheer cunning.

Although his hatred for the white man was obvious, the warrior deplored the Mexicans even more, due to the fact that his mother, wife, and children, all guiltless of any criminal doings, were killed long before by Mexican soldiers. Thus his raids south of the border were vicious and filled with fury, even as his reign of terror came to an end.

Geronimo's final surrender came on September 3, 1886, to General Nelson Miles. Evidently, he did not understand the "unconditional" clause attached to his giving up and believed he would be sent back to San Carlos, where, as soon as he mustered his strength, he could escape once again. To his horror, he found he was to be shipped to a prison in Florida.

Here he spent some time, before once again being moved, relocated to Fort Sill, Oklahoma. A broken man, the savage warrior had reverted to selling photos of himself, holding a bow and arrow, for money.

Exploiting his bloody reputation, which had been enhanced by Eastern newspapers, he was allowed to go on tour as little more than a novelty act. He was seen at Omaha's International Exposition in 1898, the Pan-American Exposition in Buffalo, New York, in 1901, and the 1904 World's Fair held at St. Louis, Missouri.

Even more incredibly, at the time of his death at Fort Sill in 1909, he was listed on the federal payroll as an army scout.

Geronimo *(Photo: Arizona Department of Library, Archives and Public Records)*

MORRIS GOLDWATER

(1852 - 1939)
Politician / Businessman

An uncle to the well-known Arizona Senator and failed presidential candidate, Barry Goldwater, this man likewise put together a lengthy career in politics.

Originally an heir to the businesses established by his father, Michael Goldwasser (the name was later changed to Goldwater), he eventually took up residence in Prescott, where he held several terms as mayor between 1879 and 1927, proving extremely popular with the people.

Among his accomplishments during this time was the promotion of many activities leading toward the modernization of the city, including a military unit, an updated waterworks system, the formation of various civic organizations, and contacts with railroading.

In the early 1880's he helped to organize a nationally-oriented Democratic party in Arizona and served as Chairman of the Central Territorial Committee. Not stopping there, he was elected to the Territorial Council in 1885, served as vice president of the State Constitutional Convention in 1910, then served as state senator from 1915-1916. When he finally did leave politics, he remained an active and energetic businessman, founding the Prescott National Bank and donating his services to other causes.

His younger brother, Baron, Barry's father, duplicated this success in Phoenix, where he was a ranking stockholder and director of the Valley Bank, as well as an investor who helped in the construction of the Arizona Biltmore Hotel.

Morris Goldwater *(Photo: Sharlot Hall Museum Library and Archives)*

Barry Goldwater—Morris Goldwater's nephew, U. S. Senator and Presidential candidate. *(Photo: Sharlot Hall Museum Library and Archives)*

DR. GEORGE GOODFELLOW

(1855 - 1910)

Doctor

Born in California, George Goodfellow later attended the U.S. Naval Academy at Annapolis, but was expelled after a fight made local headlines which carried his name.

He moved on to the University Of Wooster, in Cleveland, Ohio, where he studied medicine and graduated in 1876. Marrying shortly after obtaining his degree, he moved back West, first to California, then to Arizona, where he became a company doctor in Prescott, for his father's mine.

Later, he became an army physician, working both at Fort Whipple and Fort Lowell until 1879, when he took up private practice in Tombstone. There he became not only the town's surgeon, but the coroner as well. Aside from being a capable doctor, he also became a pioneer in early-day plastic surgery, as shown when he repaired the face of an accident victim named George Parsons in 1881, reconstructing the nose via wire and plaster beneath the skin.

Goodfellow's career was not all kindness and salvation, although he saved many people from potentially fatal gunshot and knife wounds, via surgical skills reflecting great ingenuity for the time. When outlaw John Heath was lynched in Tombstone and no one wanted to bring charges against any of the mob's members, it being the general belief the bandit received what he deserved, the good doctor came to the rescue. In his capacity as coroner, he declared the late Heath had "died from lack of breath" and the case was duly closed.

In 1900, Goodfellow moved back to California, setting up an office on Sutter Street in San Francisco. He took to writing, but continued to ply his trade as medic, too, venturing as far as Mexico and the South American continent. He died in the Angelus Hospital in Los Angeles on December 7, 1910, continuing to practice medicine until a few months before his death.

FRANK GOTCH
Wrestler

Frank Gotch *(Photo from the collection of Charles E. Gilbert)*

As the Wild West era was drawing to a close, Frank Gotch captured national fame which could have easily rivaled that of John L. Sullivan's or Gentleman Jim Corbett's in earlier boxing cycles.

Even in places where he never saw action, his exploits were accounted for in the media and his face was well-known. While this Iowa-based grappler placed emphasis on the Midwest as a homebase, he traveled the country, as many had done before him and still do to this day.

He was also a tough customer in the ring, who could tie someone in knots in no time, without the foppishness, circus-clowning, and theatrics of the "sport" as it is known today.

On Labor Day, 1911, spectators came from all over the country, paying a gate of $155,000 to see Gotch defeat George Hackenschmidt in a hard-fought bout which saw both men losing their tempers, resorting to bare-knuckle blows. The victory was only one impressive notch in a long and triumphant career.

From 1898 through 1913, he had 160 pro bouts, winning 154 of them. His last loss was on a fluke to Fred Beell during a "World Championship" bout in 1906, a defeat he quickly avenged in a rematch that same year.

While Gotch has been forgotten by most fans in the world that made him famous, overshadowed by the likes of Hulk Hogan, The Road Warriors, Ric Flair, and Dusty Rhodes, his home town of Humboldt, Iowa still remembers him. Museums and an interesting Historical Society exist in his honor.

SHARLOT HALL

(1870 - 1943)
Pioneer / Author / Historian

Sharlot Hall in the 1920's. *(Photo: Sharlot Hall Museum Library and Archives)*

One of the foremost citizens of Prescott, Arizona, Hall first came west with her parents via wagon train and lived through many of the trialsome times which earmarked Arizona for Western rowdiness.

Essentially, she experienced things as an observer, with a firm memory and amazing ability to recollect facts others would have long since forgotten.

Hall became a poet, dealing with the West and the beauty of the developing countryside, rather than the guns, glory, and gold which served as dominant themes for other writers. She also took to more extensive work, including a book which likewise dealt with the Arizona theme, and became recognized as an expert in Western culture, even though she was raised in a time period where women were traditionally kept out of the mainstream of social happenings.

It was her initiative which stirred others into maintaining the preservation of the old log cabin which had been the first governor's "mansion" in Prescott, and became active in other civic affairs. During the last territorial days, before statehood took place, she was appointed the official Historian for Arizona.

It is through Hall's personal word and writing that we know much about early-day life in the Southwest and how the pioneers got along. In modern-day Prescott, she is remembered via a museum carrying her name, which remains a top tourist attraction.

DEAF CHARLIE HANKS

(1863 - 1902)

Outlaw

Born Camilla Hanks, this stocky, violent-tempered man was called "Deaf Charlie" because of a hearing impairment which caused him to tilt his head to one side like a grotesque owl, when listening to others.

While operating much of the time out of Las Vegas, New Mexico, his criminal career covered many areas, especially after joining "The Wild Bunch." In 1892 he was arrested following the robbery of a Northern Pacific train in Montana and spent nearly a decade in jail. The prison time did little to reform or mellow the man, who returned to his life of crime in short order.

Figuring a different railroad might provide better luck, he stuck up a Great Northern train and headed south with the money, bent on ultimately returning to New Mexico. He never made it, stopping in Texas to spend some of his ill-gotten gain. This proved to be his undoing.

On October 22, 1902, he stepped into a bar in San Antonio, Texas, where he became drunk. Someone reportedly laughed at the way he tilted his head, which caused a fight to erupt, converting into an all-out brawl. Lawmen were called and in a panic, he drew his gun, knowing if he allowed himself to be arrested, he would be easily identified.

Instead, he took the option of shooting his way to freedom, but failed in his bid to do so. Shot while attempting to make his escape, he died moments later, bringing his long, but seldom profitable career as an outlaw to an end.

Curiously, almost humorously, the Pinkerton Agency which spent so much time tracking "The Wild Bunch", kept a file on Hanks, listing his "occupation" as "cowboy" and noting his "criminal occupation" beneath it as "train robber."

JOHN WESLEY HARDIN

(1853 - 1895)
Gunfighter / Outlaw

This romantic figure of the West was a drunkard, a braggart, and a psychotic killer in real life.

Although his death toll of over 40 men may have been stretching the truth considerably, he had his share of shootings, starting at the age of 15, when he killed an unarmed Negro who insulted him. The brushes with the law, gun battles, escapes, and other assorted crimes spanned several years, until he finally made an effort to retire from a life of crime.

A vindictive Texas Ranger named John Armstrong, however, was determined to see the gunman brought to justice for the killing of a deputy sheriff named Webb in a saloon brawl. This lawman tracked the killer all the way to Pollard, Alabama, where Hardin was found using a different name, while working as a timber merchant.

He somehow managed to escape the death penalty, but spent 16 years in jail. All this time behind bars allowed him to study both the law and biblical concepts. In 1894, he was released, supposedly rehabilitated.

He drifted to El Paso and there, set up practice as an attorney, but his constant drinking caused him to run off at the mouth once too often. After threatening an outlaw-turned-lawman named John Selman, he failed to realize the man was unimpressed by his reputation as a gunfighter. While drinking at the Acme Saloon on San Antonio Street, on the night of August 19, 1895, Hardin let the liquor get his guard down, enabling Selman to put a bullet through his head from behind.

Never realizing what hit him, he was killed instantly, and his body laid to rest in El Paso's Concordia Cemetery.

PEARL HART

(1878 - 1925)
Outlaw

Pistol used by
Pearl Hart.
*(Photo from the
author's collection)*

Made out to be a "bandit queen" in the tradition of Belle Starr, Pearl Hart, born Pearl Taylor in Ontario, Canada was scarcely the lady desperado the press made her out to be.

At the age of 16, she eloped with a vagrant named William Hart and headed west after realizing her marriage was doomed to failure. While working as a waitress in Mammoth, Arizona, she met a miner named Joe Boot, with whom she formed an ill-fated partnership, aimed at robbing stagecoaches.

On May 30, 1899, they held up the Benson-Globe stage, but were quickly captured, due to the bungling nature in which they'd carried out their crime. Hart received a five-year sentence and Boot was hit with a whopping thirty five years at the territorial prison in Yuma.

This poverty-program Belle Starr served two years of her sentence before meeting parole, then took her act on the road for a short spell, appearing in theatres across the country. Often-reproduced photographs showed her decked out in outlaw attire, holding a variety of weapons, although it is suspect whether she'd ever fired one in real life or knew how to shoot.

In 1905 she again tried to make it as a bandit, robbing a train, but being released for lack of evidence. Afterward, she dropped out of sight, most likely changing her name and going into hiding.

In 1924 she supposedly resurfaced briefly, visiting the Pima County jail where she was once held, identifying herself, taking a look around, then quickly fleeing. After that, not much is known of her fate.

WILLIAM S. HART

(1870 - 1946)

Film Star

Born William Surray Hart, this New Yorker grew up in South Dakota, where Sioux Indian influence was strong, making him more than routinely familiar with the West of old.

When silent film became the rage, he put this knowledge into practice, becoming a major box office attraction in the Western genre. Among his credits were "The Bargain," "The Narrow Trail," "The Toll Gate," "Blue Blazes," and several others.

Notably violent for its time was another movie called "Hell's Hinges," which Clint Eastwood stole some scenes from and revamped later into his "High Plains Drifter," decades after the Hart classic had slipped from public view.

As far as Western stars were concerned, Hart was not the unrealistic, overly-heroic, do-gooder as portrayed by contemporaries of his time and imitators who would come later, as singing, swinging, smiling sharpshooters. Hart, on the contrary, gained recognition for the gloominess of his face, his unwillingness to crack a smile except in rare circumstances, and for aiming to kill, rather than disable or shoot the gun from the hand of an antagonist.

He was, in short, a mock hero, probably much closer in character to the real gunfighters and lawmen of the West, than any other hyped-up screen actor's characterization.

In 1922, Hart decided to call it quits with the film world and retired to his ranch, where he lived the life of an actual cowboy. He died in 1946.

JOHN HEATH

(18?? - 1884)
Gambler / Outlaw

Little was recorded about John Heath prior to his arrival in Bisbee, Arizona, where he gained a job as a faro dealer in a saloon.

On December 8, 1883, a group of masked men robbed the Goldwater-Castaneda store of a payroll, but the hold-up went haywire, the gang members blasting their guns at anything that moved as they made their escape. When a hunting party was formed to track down the bandits who had left dead bodies behind them, including a woman who had been watching the spectacle from a window, Heath offered his services as a tracker.

The chase was on, but the vigilantes were misled along the wrong path, while the killers got away. It was later discovered that Heath was the actual leader of the whole band, had helped plan the robbery, and although not anticipating the killings, intended from the start to lead the posse astray.

Eventually the other participants in the robbery, Dan Dowd, Red Sample, Tex Howard, William Delaney and Dan Kelley were captured, receiving the death sentence. Since Heath had not actually pulled a trigger, he was given life in prison.

On February 22, 1884, a group of angry Bisbee citizens rode down to Tombstone, where Heath was being held. Breaking him out of jail, they lynched him from a telegraph pole.

This pole has long since been removed, but a marker still stands, indicating the spot where the surprise execution took place. No arrests were ever made in this example of mob justice and the incident was brushed over.

On March 8th of that same year, his accomplices met death by hanging, legally. Their graves all rest in Tombstone's Boot Hill Cemetery, and, while to a man, they proclaimed their innocence, all evidence points to the contrary.

JAMES HOGG

(1851 - 1906)
Politician / Businessman

While his name might sound like satire, James Hogg was in fact, a popular politician from Texas, who stood more for the people than his own self-interest.

He made several enemies during his career, due to his relentless attacking of the railroad industry, which he branded an enemy to the farmers, the working class, and the poor people of his state.. During the 1890's, his reign as governor was marked with controversy, yet the portly politician remained the Democratic party's prize possession.

His securing of a railroad commission law in 1891 further alienated him from the powerful train industry. However, he gained the support of the common people, who viewed the railways as trespassing giants and plunderers. While unquestionably well-intentioned and energetic, Hogg's ideals sometimes bordered on fanaticism and may have hindered the growth of his state in the long run.

Radical, almost militant in his thirst for reform, the main criticism of his policies lies in his zeal for upholding local interests, over the national economy and the country as a whole. Whether he was good, bad, or somewhere in between would be a matter of question.

Upon leaving politics, Hogg invested in the oil industry and made a fortune. Up to the point of his death in 1906, he continued to be outspoken in thought and deed, even though he no longer held public office.

A colorful, unpredictable individual, there was no in-between concerning public opinion. He was either utterly loved or entirely hated by those around him.

DOC HOLLIDAY

(1852 - 1887)

Gambler / Drunkard
Gunfighter / Dentist

When tuberculosis caused this Georgia-born dentist to disband his practice in favor of the more lucrative profession of gambler, a legend was born.

Ill-tempered, hard-drinking, and murderous, John Henry Holliday's trail spanned through Texas, Colorado, New Mexico, Kansas, and Arizona. Sometimes operating on the side of the law, sometimes running from it, he became one of the most puzzling people to ever emerge in the Wild West.

While his reputed fast draw and number of verified kills may have been more myth than fact, he was still undisputably violent in nature, seeing death as a great settling element for arguments more often than not. He remained somewhat of a playboy, in spite of his alcoholism, constant cough, and fighting attitude.

His romancing of Kate Elder, who claimed to be his "wife" although no indication exists they were ever actually married, ranks as his best known love affair, although several others took place, including some torrid sessions with a red-haired lady gambler named Lottie Deno.

It was in Arizona that Doc stepped into legend. Although accused of robbing a stagecoach in cooperation with his supposed arch-enemies, the Clantons, and possibly even Wyatt Earp, most books have him billed as a "good guy" during this phase of his life.

Assisting the Earps in the notorious OK Corral gunfight, he was slightly wounded, but managed to kill or at least help kill both McLowery Brothers and 19-year-old Billy Clanton. The bullets and blood did not stop with this shoot-out, but escalated.

When Virgil Earp was wounded in ambush and Morgan Earp was killed in a pool hall, Wyatt intended to see justice served, with or without legal grounds to do so. Holliday again pitched in, eager to do battle. After supposedly helping to kill a

Clanton Ranch employee, Florentino Cruz, who was suspected as one of the gunmen during the aforementioned attacks against the Earps, Holliday fled to Colorado.

Attempts were made to bring him back to Arizona to stand trial for murder, but Governor Pitkin refused to return the homicidal dentist to Tombstone. For a brief time, he drifted to Deadwood in the Dakotas, returning to Colorado on account of the cold weather, which he felt worsened his cough.

Settling in Leadville, he came upon increasingly hard times. His last shooting victim was an off-duty policeman named A.J. Kelly, following an argument. Doc pleaded self-defense and again went free.

In the spring of 1887, he entered a sanatorium at Glenwood Springs, Colorado. On November 8 of that year, he died in bed, shortly after downing a glass of whiskey. Knowing he was about to die and having claimed he would never leave this world with his boots off, he ordered those around him to put them on. With a curse uttered under his breath, the legendary gunfighting dentist passed from this world into the next, in the condition he dreaded most of all.

Doc Holliday, gunman, card-cheat, killer, gambler, outlaw, dentist, womanizer, drunkard, saloon owner, and a host of other things, died with his boots off! Oddly enough, some time beforehand, his spasmodic lover, Kate Elder, died the death he would have preferred, from a gunshot wound in a bar.

TEMPLE HOUSTON

(1860 - 1905)

Lawyer / Gunfighter

The long-haired son of Sam Houston worked as a cattle driver and a page boy in the U.S. Senate, before studying law to become an effective attorney.

He evidently knew firearms as well as legal documents, demonstrating this art at numerous times in his life, mainly as a sharpshooter rather than a gunman. He once won a shooting contest against Billy The Kid, according to unsubstantiated gossip, and was a friend of gun-toting Bat Masterson.

On one instance, however, he put his abilities with a gun into physical play. This took place on October 7, 1894, against two fellow lawyers, Ed and John Jennings. In the end, Houston killed the former and seriously wounded the other, leaving no doubt in anyone's mind about his capacities as an actual gunfighter, if called upon to be one.

After the showdown, two other Jennings boys, Al and Frank, who were likewise attorneys, disgraced their father, a prominent judge, by turning to outlawry, figuring it to be safer than practicing law in Texas.

Houston died from natural causes in Woodward, Texas, rather than by gunfire as might have been predicted following his shootout with the Jennings clan.

During his latter years, while still reading and studying law, he developed a second pastime, weaving rattlesnake-skin ties.

GEORGE HUNT

(1859 - 1934)
Politician

This bald, walrus-like, cartoonish character was perhaps the most popular political personality in the history of old Arizona.

While comical and dull-looking by appearance, he was in fact, a cunning and intelligent human being, proven by the fact that when he first arrived in Globe, he was all but penniless, riding in on a mule, in hope of finding work. Within two decades, he built a fortune, honestly too, which was even more of an accomplishment, concerning mass-corruption in most phases of the business and political world at the time.

Hunt became the first governor of the new "state" of Arizona, after territorial status was lifted, and served multiple terms from 1912 through 1933, under the Democratic banner. During the bulk of this time, his most furious opponent was the Republican hardliner Thomas Campbell.

Their 1917 election race was one of the most controversial in the history of politics, with Hunt insisting on a number of recounts until finally, he was given the victory, after a long, circus-like ordeal. At one point, Campbell had been declared governor, served a stormy 11 months, then was removed, with Hunt thrown in to finish the term which was rightfully his.

This charming man could deceive people with his small-town, small-time, old-country-boy charm, too, as some of his campaign tactics demonstrated. One of his shrewdest strategies was to keep files on people he met during travel or tours to secure votes, then, when he planned to return to these areas, he would draw from this home-library.

Supposedly able to wow his contacts with a memory of super-human skills, the people he spoke to were stunned that he remembered their names, their professions, and obscure facts from their last conversation. No one bothered to think this was not from keen mental storage, but a series of fact books kept at hand and studied before coming to town.

Likewise, the recipient of complimentary gifts during the campaign trail didn't always get what he or she bargained for. One of Hunt's favorite tactics was to buy up great quantities of jam from the stores, remove the labels from the jars, and hand out "home-made" jellies his wife had supposedly made, but in truth never touched, to various influential people.

Prior to his death, Hunt was active in other areas besides the governorship. He had worked as a waiter, a store clerk, a miner, and a laborer in his youth. In his old age, he served a brief stint as an ambassador in Siam. He was also active in the El Zaribah Shrine, his shriner's cap being one of the many exhibits on display at the Arizona State Capitol Museum in Phoenix.

His tomb may also be seen in that city, atop a hill in the vicinity of the local zoo. It is a small, white pyramid, surrounded by a black fence, an unusual grave, marking the life's accomplishments of a colorful and unusual man.

George W. P. Hunt, first governor of Arizona *(Photo: Sharlot Hall Museum Library and Archives)*

Gov. Hunt's tomb on hillside near Phoenix Zoo. *(Photo by the author)*

JOHN ILIFF

(1831 - 1878)

Cattleman

Born in McLuney, Ohio and educated at Ohio Wesleyan University, Iliff rejected the life of a farmer. He decided to put his education to good use in the slowly developing West.

What started out as a minor business venture eventually developed into a booming empire. His 1859 settlement near Cherry Creek, Colorado, exploded into a cattle kingdom covering a range over 150 miles long on the South Platte River.

This, too, proved to be a calculated strategy on his part, enabling him to control water rights which further increased both his power and his fortune. At one point it was said he could travel from Greeley to Julesburg and still not be out of contact with his numerous ranch houses. It was also estimated he owned up to 50,000 head of cattle or more during his best years.

In spite of the dubious reputation other land barons and cattlemen had, Iliff maintained an attitude of honesty throughout his life, rare in this particular time period. After his death, he was praised by many as a level-headed and trustworthy man who, incredibly, made a fortune without stealing or killing to get it.

The Methodist Iliff School of Theology, on the campus of the University of Denver, remains as one tribute to this enterprising businessman's contributions to the West.

Perhaps this cattle baron's honest practices stems from his heavily religious upbringing from birth. His full name was John Wesley Iliff, derived from John Wesley, the founder of the Wesleyan Church, the denomination in which he was raised.

CALVIN JAMES

(18?? - 1886)
Whisky Runner
Outlaw / Killer

Curiously, Calvin James was a gang leader operating between Arkansas and Texas in a big-time business selling liquor in the Indian Nations. It was while plying this trade that he overstepped himself, carrying out the crime that led to his downfall.

In the summer of 1885, he and his partners made a large whiskey purchase in Texas. As he was returning through the Chickasaw Nation, he shot one of his associates, Tony Love, then turned his weapon upon fellow businessmen, Henry Robey and Albert Kemp, evidently intent on keeping all the liquor, plus profits, for himself.

Realizing he was outnumbered, he decided against his original plan, choosing to make peace with the other two, then hid Love's body in some bushes, claiming he would kill either man if they talked.

Covering up the crime was not so simple. Other parties knew this gang well and when Love was not seen among them, the suspicions grew strong that somewhere along the trail, he had been done away with. James, Robey, and Kemp were arrested, the latter two agreeing to testify against the gang leader as government witnesses.

Due to this, the outlaw was quickly convicted and sentenced to death. On July 23, 1886, he died on the gallows as part of a double-event execution with another killer named Lincoln Sprole. The hanging, as customary in those days, was attended by a large throng of onlookers who came to see the liquor peddler who had tried to do in his own partners take the long drop.

It seemed fitting justice that James, a double-crosser of the first order, was betrayed and convicted by the two very same men he originally intended to kill out of greed.

JEREZANO

(1867 - 1912)

Bullfighter

Born Manuel Lara, he took the stage name of Jerezano because he came from Jerez De La Frontera, Spain.

He offered one particularly good performance in Madrid on September 8, 1896, but otherwise gained only modest recognition in Europe, in spite of a long career before the bulls.

In Mexico, however, he proved to be a phenomenon, building a massive following for himself spanning from the border to the interior. Each spring and summer he struggled to make a name for himself in his native Spain, then spent the winter months in Mexico, enjoying uncanny star status. It was on one such Mexican tour that he met an unexpected and highly unorthodox end.

On October 6, 1912, he appeared for the final time in Veracruz and as he worked an animal from the ranch of Nopalapan, the beast veered away from the cape and slammed him to the ground. Although ungored, he received a violent blow from the flat of the horn, which caused unchecked internal damage. Failing to realize the seriousness of his condition, he returned to the Hotel Universal in the city, where he ruptured, developed peritonitis, and died two days following the fatal bullfight.

While history accounts for many matadors dying from gorings in the heart, lung, or neck, Jerezano enjoys the dubious distinction of being one of the few to become a victim of the bulls, without the horn even penetrating his flesh.

The bullfighter's body was returned to Spain for burial, where the appropriate obituaries appeared and he quickly became a forgotten face in the pages of history books. For a short time, however, he enjoyed distinction in Latin America as one of the Wild West's bravest matadors.

Still going strong in his 40's, he had passed the age at which most others retire and might have continued well into the 1920's, had the bulls not decided otherwise.

JOHNNY BEHIND THE DEUCE

(18?? - ????)
Gambler

Johnny Behind The Deuce, an obvious alias, was a mystery man back in his own time and remains so now, as so little is known about him.

He drifted into Charleston, Arizona in 1880 and quickly set himself up as somewhat of a teenage gambling sensation at the various card tables. In January of 1881, however, he became engaged in a loud dispute with a mining engineer named Henry Schneider, over a supposed burglary.

The miner pulled a knife, the gambler pulled a gun, and with this knowledge in mind, the winner of the exchange becomes easy to figure. Schneider was buried. Johnny was jailed, still refusing to give his real name or any background information.

Miners wanted to form a lynch mob, which saw the youthful card player hustled about for his own safety. He was sent first to Tombstone, then Tucson, where he escaped from jail and was never recaptured. What happened to this shadowy character afterward remains based upon conjecture.

Some people have contended Johnny went to Mexico and never crossed the line into America again. Others insist he went back to being whoever or whatever he was before his Arizona arrival and lived a normal life in the East. Others, still, insist he was the "Mike O'Rourke" later killed by Pony Deal in Sulphur Springs, Arizona, during the winter of 1882.

Whatever the case may be, Johnny Behind The Deuce became somewhat of a bogeyman to the people of Arizona, particularly in mining camps, where his victim was remembered and people fumed over not seeing his card-turning killer hanged.

JACK JOHNSON

(1878 - 1946)

Boxer

The first black man to hold the World Heavyweight Boxing Championship, Jack Johnson might not be considered by some as a figure from Wild West times, but his career, spanning from 1899 to 1924 certainly qualifies him for inclusion.

While he might not have been a permanent resident of the West, he certainly visited there enough, where his name was well-known, hated by some, loved by others. In some towns, such as Reno, Nevada, where he tromped all over aging has-been, Jim Jeffries, signs were posted throughout the outdoor arena, that all guns had to be checked, for fear someone would shoot the black man if he gained a victory over the popular "white hope" he was matched against.

Johnson's professional and personal life remained torn with controversy. A fugitive in the U.S.A. who was forced to fight outside America over indictment on the Mann Act, he further infuriated the public by marrying a white woman, an act unheard of at the time, flaunting an overblown life-style at every chance he got.

His boxing career was likewise a rollercoaster ride. While he thrashed numerous opponents, charges and confessions to fixed fights plagued him. When he finally lost his belt to Jess Willard in Havana, Cuba, charges of "taking a dive" flew up almost immediately. A much-talked-about photograph shows the fallen champion on his back, not dazed, but evidently stretching his arms over his head to shield out the sun.

Such was not the first time accusations were made concerning the integrity of his matches.

Even earlier, Johnson was to "carry" a mediocre, but popular tough guy named Stan Ketchel in a much-hyped bout. Ketchel evidently decided to doublecross the black man, flooring him with an unexpected punch in the 12th round. Luckily for Johnson, but unluckily for Ketchel, the punch

Jack Johnson *(Photo courtesy Lew Eskin)*

scored a knockdown but not a knockout. Johnson got up, showing obvious rage, flattened Ketchel, then leaned on the ropes and stared down disgustedly at him, with a hand on his hip, while the 10 count was delivered.

During the era when "The Wild Bunch" was being killed off to a man and the few survivors fleeing, Jack Johnson started a career as a boxer. While Pancho Villa was winning headlines as a revolutionary, this towering black hulk was making waves as a love-hate celebrity in the world of fisticuffs. While the gunfighters and lawmen captured their moment in the history of the West, Jack Johnson became a standout in the world of sports.

On June 10, 1946, he was killed in a car crash. During his final years he had mellowed somewhat, seeking ways to make up for his past, wild lifestyle. He had wanted to help a number of charities, through the assistance of his old manager, Dan Morgan, but died before most of these could come about.

JOHN JONES

(1829 - 1912)
Businessman / Politician

Born in England, John Jones arrived in America with his migrating parents while still an infant, settling near Cleveland, Ohio.

The California Gold Rush first attracted his attention in 1850 and lured him west, where he became a prospector, deputy sheriff, and politician. He also became a cunning businessman who started investing in mines, rather than digging for minerals himself.

Still holding high political hopes for himself, he drifted into Nevada where he figured his ambitions for public office would be more easily met. This again proved a calculating adventure, as he became a senator in the 1870's and continued a successful reign for several years.

He retired in 1903, having firmly established himself as a statesman and well-liked spokesman for the people. During this lengthy time span, he shifted his interests from gold, which originally brought him from the East, to silver and while much of the legislation his campaign supported might have been based on personal interests, these corresponded with the general opinions of Nevadans, many of whom relied on the silver trade for their livelihood.

After retirement, the aging political figurehead devoted his energies to an easier life, enjoying the profits from land developments, real estate investments, and mining. He died in 1912.

Jones, incidentally, founded the town of Santa Monica, California, in 1875, another of the accomplishments marking his life.

BLACKJACK KETCHUM

(1867 - 1901)
Outlaw

The life of Tom "Blackjack" Ketchum could have easily passed for something out of a script for "My Name Is Nobody," "Blazing Saddles," or some other mediocre Western comedy, proving reality stranger than fiction in the case of this peculiar badman.

He talked to himself, he talked to walls, he talked to the sky, most likely hearing answers within his mind as well. Evidently aware of his own mental shortcomings, he had a habit of correcting himself after doing something stupid.

Often, he was seen hitting himself in the head with his pistol, while muttering such things as, "Oh, will you, now? Is that so? Take that, and that, and that!" When these self-administered pistol-whippings weren't enough, he used other measures, as in the case where he lost a girl he loved to another man. Rather than feeling hatred for the woman, he went down to a river bank and started beating himself with a knotted saddle rope, stopping only after being restrained by friends.

In spite of such odd behavior, some people saw the quality of leadership in this fellow, helping him form a gang of robbers, but most of their activities were laughably bungled. This was not to say Ketchum was a complete court jester, to be taken lightly on all accounts, for he had a mean temperament and although he denied ever killing anyone, evidence points to the contrary.

His affiliation with such outlaw notables as Butch Cassidy and "The Wild Bunch" also remains documented, this association stemming from his vastly overblown reputation as a wicked outlaw. When eventually captured and sentenced to death, he relished the publicity he received and his weird behavior grew even more obvious.

Ranting and raving, he stated several times how he not

only expected to go to hell for his crimes, but looked forward to the trip. He wrote a letter to the youth of America, not steering them away from crime, but suggesting if they had to become criminals, they should investigate the career of train robber over other, more petty crimes, and kill anyone getting in their way.

Daily, he watched the scaffold being prepared from his cell window, commenting on what he thought was good work. He even requested violin music be played when he took the drop. Such antics became the talk of New Mexico, as the public eagerly awaited the fatal day to arrive. Was Blackjack really as unafraid to die as he claimed or would he crack, proving himself a coward as the noose was fastened around his neck?

On April 26, 1901, the big day came, Ketchum once again thriving on the attention he received. Muttering to himself as usual, he trotted pleasantly up the 13 steps to the trap door, which he leaped upon as if to perform a tap dance. "Let her go," was the last statement he was to utter before the hood was placed over his head and his request was carried out. An inexperienced executioner botched the job, his miscalculations in weight causing the ill-fated bandit to be decapitated from the force of the fall.

Thus Blackjack Ketchum died as he lived, even failing to hang properly.

PETER LASSEN

(1793 - 1859)
Pioneer / Prospector / Politician

Born in Copenhagen, Peter Lassen migrated to America in 1822, spending several years in the East before moving westward.

In 1844, he received a 26,000 acre land grant in California's Sacramento Valley, which he quickly attempted to colonize and ranch upon, founding a town called Benton.

In 1849, the gold rush hit, driving him north to Shasta, where along with a postmaster named Isaac Roop, he planned to form yet another colony as he had done with Benton. When a fire destroyed Shasta in 1853, he and his partner found the excuse they'd been waiting for.

Heading toward the California/Utah border, they organized a group of settlers on 33,000 square acres of land. This area they named Nataqua, which roughly encompassed a third of present-day Nevada.

This location was eventually reorganized to become the territory of Sierra Nevada, and in 1861, after Lassen's death, the territory of Nevada. After serving a brief stint as the first territorial governor of the Sierra Nevada territory, Lassen decided to seek further adventure, a decision which caused his death.

In 1859, having gone to search for gold along the Oregon-California border, he was ambushed by Indians and killed. Mount Lassen, Lassen Volcanic National Park, and Lassen County in California, were all named in his honor.

His exploits have also become legendary within the history of Freemasonry, as he, like many other western figureheads, was a member.

HARPER LEE

(1884 - 1941)
Bullfighter

At the turn of the century, Harper Lee began his career in the bullrings of Mexico.

First considered a novelty, he later became a favorite of Mexican and American audiences alike. He also enjoyed the distinction of being the first U.S. citizen to become a matador de toros.

During an impressive career, Lee appeared several times in the Mexican interior, including Aguascalientes, Zacatecas, Mexico City, Puebla, and Guanajuato. His best showings were in the north, however, closer to the border. Torreon, Nuevo Loredo, Juarez, and Monterrey were locations where he did well.

Many spectators who scoffed at the idea of an American bullfighter were stunned with the courage he displayed, including a continual execution of the "cambio de rodillas," a pass done on both knees. The Texas-born torero likewise competed with or even outshined Frutitos, Francisco Alonso (the father of actor Gilbert Roland), Mazzantinito, Cuatro Dedos, and other well-known performers at the time.

He was seriously gored three times as a professional, the worst in Saltillo, on October 15, 1911. It was after that he decided to retire, eventually founding a chicken ranch.

Suffering from cancer, he died on June 26, 1941 and although he'd wanted to be cremated, his wife refused the second part of his request, which was to have his ashes scattered over San Antonio. Instead, these remains were buried in the Mission Cemetery of that town, the headstone reading Harper B. Gillett (his real name), 1884-1941, with no mention of his bullfighting career.

BILL LONGELY

(1851 - 1877)
Gunfighter

Negro-hating psychopath, quick-tempered bully and out-law, Bill Longely established himself in Texas as a dangerous man, to be avoided by all comers if possible.

This reputation was enhanced when he started killing blacks for no reason, including a policeman in Houston, which sent him on the run. Eventually, his fleeing from the law caused him to cross his own, personally-established color barrier, attacking and robbing whites as well.

At that point, even the segment of bigots and white supremacists who had backed his killing of minorities, turned against him, leaving him totally without support. Realizing there was no turning back, he continued to plunder and kill, operating on the assumption this was the life he would lead until capture.

His reign of terror spread to Utah, where he shot a soldier in Salt Lake City, but was captured shortly afterward and sent to the Fort Leavenworth stockade in Kansas. Two years later he escaped or was released, depending on which of two conflicting sources is to be believed and completely unreformed, went about killing again.

Returning to Texas, his crime spree lasted through 1876, when he once again found himself plagued by lawmen. He went to Louisiana, hid, got caught, and was transfered to Texas once more. This time, the government decided to put a permanent damper on his actions.

On October 11, 1877, Bill Longely was hanged in the town of Giddings. Reportedly, he made a remark to the effect that this had always been his fancied way to die. His twisted dream became reality in short order.

MANGAS COLORADAS

(1795 - 1863)

Indian leader

A gigantic Apache warrior, Mangas Coloradas first seemed interested only in attacking Mexicans, prior to an incident with the white men that turned him into a brutal, bloodthirsty hater of whites.

The offending action, known as The Picnic Massacre, occurred in 1837, when the Apaches were invited to a feast in Santa Rita del Cobre, Arizona. The scenario was set up by notorious scalphunter, John Johnson, who exploded a bomb while the Indians ate and drank, then set out to demolish the survivors with knives, pistols, and howitzers.

Over 400 Apaches were killed, including an important chief named Juan Jose, but Mangas was one of the lucky few to escape. From that point on, he launched an all-out vendetta against everyone and anyone who was not a member of his tribe.

In 1851 he broke a short-lasting peace pact with the whites, which he'd made on a temporary basis during the Mexican-American War, and once again embarked on a path of pillage and destruction. His reign of terror continued until 1862, when he was wounded in battle and taken to Janos, Mexico, for treatment.

Geronimo, who was with him at the time, gave the doctors an ultimatum that certainly made the Indian leader's recovery in their best interest. "Make well. If he die, so does everyone in Janos!" This bit of persuasion was all the medics needed to save the life of Mangas Coloradas, although his injuries took their toll on him.

Some time later, still weak and worn, he decided it was time to talk peace. On January 17, 1863, he surrendered at an army camp near Fort McLean. Here, for the final time, he was double-crossed by the white men.

Officially shot while attempting to escape, evidence points to the fact he was tortured by being tied down and burned by hot bayonets, before being stabbed and shot to death. His brain was also supposedly removed for surgical study and the body butchered beyond recognition.

JOSEPHINE MARCUS

(1862 - 1944)
Housewife

The daughter of prominent Jewish merchants, Josephine Sarah Marcus became the final love of the down-on-his-luck Wyatt Earp, who had lost his previous wife through death by natural causes in 1888.

Awestruck by the aging gunman, she fell in love and the two were married in 1898. Afterward, they headed for Alaska, where Wyatt established a gambling hall, before realizing the venture was not a sound one.

In 1901, they returned to California and continued to live as a happy couple in spite of various trials. They had two children, but neither lived to adulthood. Likewise, Wyatt's antics and varied schemes to make money, legally or illegally, rubbed his more virtuous spouse the wrong way on various occasions, but she remained faithful until the old lawman died in January of 1929.

Fearing retaliation from old enemies or relic-hunting Wild West enthusiasts, she and other family members kept the burial site of her husband's cremated ashes a closely guarded secret.

Many years later an unidentified party found the location, stealing the huge headstone. By that time, however, Josephine too, had long since passed on, dying in 1944.

While Wyatt's exploits grew to be legendary, Josephine's loyalty and very existence were ignored by writers and film people alike, until the early 1980's when a movie called "I Married Wyatt Earp" hit the television screens. Josephine was played by Marie Osmond.

BAT MASTERSON

(1853 - 1921)
Gunfighter / Gambler

Born Bartholomew Masterson, in Quebec, Canada, he later legally changed his name to William Barkley Masterson, but readily accepted the "Bat" nickname most of his life.

A buffalo hunter, gambler, lawman, and gunfighter, he was not the total good guy comic books have made him out to be, but was not completely bad either. During the 1870's and 1880's, he drifted through Colorado, Kansas, Texas, Arizona, and other locations, plying various trades.

His reputation as a fast-draw became well-known, but somewhat disputable. Few screenwriters have ever mentioned the fact that he was not always deadly with his guns. In 1876, he was caught up in a fight over a dance hall girl, killing a military officer named King, but was wounded badly in the process.

In 1881, he fought a duel with Al Updegraph, missing his mark and only grazing the man. For this, he received a fine of $10 and was ordered to pay the victim's medical bill. All this hardly befits the image of a deadly pistolero history has tagged on to him.

As the 1900's rolled around, Masterson was caught up in unsavory gambling scandals and decided to leave the West, which was changing anyway. He moved to New York, where, of all things, he took a job as a newspaperman.

He died of a heart attack in October of 1921, having changed his questionable skills as a gunman for even more questionable skills as a journalist.

DAVID MATHER

(1845 - ??)

Gambler / Lawman / Outlaw

David Mather, coming from the same bloodline as Puritan theologian Cotton Mather, was a direct contradiction to the religiously loyal kinsmen from his family past.

A gambler, swindler, wise-cracking prankster, and alcoholic, he sometimes worked on the side of the law, but bent it, too, when times were hard. Stories abound concerning his swindles, most notably how he and Wyatt Earp once conspired to sell fake "gold bricks" to moronic cowboys.

Another incident tells of how, when attending a church service, the minister devoted an entire sermon to saving his soul. As the services concluded, he stood up, announced he was repenting of his evil ways, stated he was ready to go to heaven now, drew his gun, and asked if any other Christians wished to make the trip with him. No one did, for when he started firing at the roof, the rest of the parishioners jumped out of the windows.

Mather engaged in several shoot-outs spanning New Mexico, Kansas, Colorado, and Texas. A brief stint as lawman in El Paso proved unfruitful, leading him to resign his position of assistant marshal over a wage dispute.

He switched to the more profitable job of pimp, but was shot by one of his whores when he tried to pocket her finances. The last facts concerning him surfaced in 1885, back in Kansas, where he was wounded in a gunfight after being accused of cheating at cards, which he most likely was. He killed one of his accusers, shot two others with superficial injuries, and was promptly sent packing as an alternative to jail.

Gossip abounds as to what may have happened to him since then, all unproven. Presumedly, he changed his name and tried to establish himself in places where he was unknown, as an honest citizen. Some say he resurfaced in Nevada, or, up in Canada, where he wormed his way into the police department, but, again, no confirmation of this exists.

When, where, or how David Mather finally died is anybody's guess.

RICHARD McCORMICK

(1832 - 1901)
Politician

Richard McCormick might be best noted as Arizona's second territorial governor, serving under the Republican banner in 1865-1869.

While this might paint a picture of triumph and happiness, such was not always the case for this man who suffered more than his share of tragedy. Among his other, more light-hearted activities, however, were the designs for the first territorial seal, the distinction of giving the town of Prescott its name, and, later, serving as a delegate to Washington.

The sadness. That came, too. Shortly after Prescott was founded and McCormick had settled down, he sent for his wife to travel from the East to be at his side. The woman, named Margaret, survived the long trip painlessly enough, but died along with her stillborn child in 1867.

Both mother and infant were buried in the woods outside Prescott, just one day prior to her 24th birthday, an equally sad and sobering fact. Some of the family artifacts, including a series of decorations she'd made, may be seen at Prescott's Sharlot Hall Museum.

Among McCormick's labors while in politics were designs for better roads, schools, and medical facilities in not only his city of residence, but the territory as a whole. He also worked to interest mining companies, farmers, developers, and railroaders in extending their services to central Arizona.

In an area rapidly filling with violent men and crooks, he did his best to speak for and protect honest citizens.

FRANK McLOWERY

(18?? - 1881)
Rancher / Outlaw

Little is recorded about Frank McLowery or his younger brother, Tom, barring the fact that both died in the OK Corral gunfight.

Alternative spelling of the family name exists as McLaury, with hints of McLowery as an alias and vice-versa. It is McLowery that first appeared on the grave of both men, so this might best be presumed as the truthful family name. Again, though, who can be certain? Still another account spells the name as McLowry, while another says McLaurie.

A former cowhand, Frank established a ranch south of Tombstone, Arizona, where with his brother, he was reputed to engage in low-key rustling activities. His friendship with Ike Clanton and other area outlaws adds credit to these charges. It also led to his death.

In 1881, a feud was brewing between the Earps, who supposedly represented law and order in Tombstone, and the outlaw factions of the McLowery-Clanton ranches. On October 26, 1881, tempers exploded when the Earps and Doc Holliday confronted the cowboys, noting they were carrying guns in town, which was against the law. Rather than surrendering their weapons, someone opened fire and the most famous duel in history was underway.

In the process, Frank took a wound that ended his life and while the shot was actually fired by "who knows" in the party, Wyatt Earp later took credit. Earp even admitted aiming at Frank first, on the premise of his being a reputed crack-shot, while his younger brother, Tom, had never claimed to kill anyone.

Frank McLowery now rests in Boot Hill along with the other fatalities of that autumn afternoon, after being given a lavish funeral bankrolled by Ike Clanton to turn the city against the Earps. The burial program included the exhibition of the dead men, under a sign saying they had been murdered on the streets of Tombstone, an argument not everyone was quick to buy.

This accusation, however, still reads as part of the epitaph on the grave.

Controversy still reigns over the spelling of the names of the OK Corral victims. The graves of the "McLowery" brothers were noted originally as such on the markers, but were changed later to McLaury to match public opinion in modern times. Debate over whether it's McLowery, McLaury, or McLaurie still runs rampant. *(Photo taken at Tombstone's Boothill Cemetery by the author)*

TOM McLOWERY

(18?? - 1881)
Rancher / Outlaw

Like his older brother, Frank, Tom McLowery's history remains cloudy.

Just how much of the illegal activity he engaged in surrounding the family ranch is questionable, his function mainly being as a "front man" who handled the legitimate end of business, while others dabbled in rustling. While Frank may have helped Old Man Clanton carry out his brutal muletrain robbery, which left many innocents dead, and was known as a sharpshooter, Tom supposedly never killed anyone.

At the time of the gunfight in which he lost his life, he was supposedly unarmed, wearing no gunbelt, but was going for a rifle holstered in his horse's saddle, as he was shot dead.

Seeing his brother fall, he decided he was next in line and decided to make a stand of it. According to legend, he went for the rifle, shouting "I've got you now" in the direction of Wyatt Earp and Doc Holliday. To this, the latter supposedly responded with a shotgun blast that nearly tore his assailant in half, answering with a sarcastic, "I don't believe you have!"

Survivors of the gunfight, namely Ike Clanton and Billy Claiborne, who had avoided death by running from the scene once the shooting started, insisted Tom had been unarmed when he was shot, throwing up his hands in the position of surrender.

The nature of his wound, however, is not the one of a man positioning himself at another's mercy, but of someone grabbing a rifle, with the intention of putting it into use, a point modern historians admit to as readily as historians of the past, who failed to believe McLowery was an innocent by-stander.

ELWOOD MEAD

(1858 - 1936)
Water & Irrigation Expert

Born to farming parents in Indiana, Elwood Mead grew up to be a land surveyor and eventually devoted his time to the study of water, particularly the irrigating of desert soil.

With a degree in engineering, he took on added responsibilities as a school teacher, placing an emphais on the instruction of agricultural techniques. During the late 1880's, he migrated to Wyoming and remained there for several years, doing survey work.

He survived the decline of the "Wild West" and its conversion to a more civilized environment without the conflicts or hostilities other white-collared newcomers faced, capitalizing upon the change in the times rather than deploring them. It was in this era of the "New West" that he made his best-known accomplishments.

In 1917, he resettled in California, where he took an extended interest in dams. In the years to come, he mounted excessive campaigns for the construction of Hoover Dam and the Grand Coulee project, with eventual success. The water impounded from this project was named Lake Mead, in homage to the man who made the allegedly "impossible" Hoover Dam construction a reality, while serving on the Bureau of Reclamation.

Such was a fitting tribute to this visionary who spent his entire life studying ways to improve farming, irrigation, and waterways in the United States. He died of natural causes in 1936.

DEACON JIM MILLER

(1866 - 1909)

Professional Killer

To call James P. Miller a "gunfighter" would be an injustice, as he was little more than a psychotic murderer, completely unlike the stereotyped pistolero who faced his enemies with a determined glare, ready to do battle or die.

This man was more comfortable shooting unarmed men from a distance, usually hidden behind a rock or tree, with a rifle blast used to bring down his prey. He was called "Deacon Jim" because he dressed like a traveling minister, claimed to embrace Christianity, and was an avid church-goer who quoted the Bible, when not busy elsewhere, doing someone in.

Killing his first victims, all family members, while still a child, he embarked early on a life of crime and murder.

While operating a hotel in Pecos, Texas, and carrying on with a feigned air of respectability, his Jekyll & Hyde personality soon manifested itself once again. He got tangled up in a feud with a lawman, Bud Frazer, whom he eventually killed with a shotgun in Toyah, when he spotted his old enemy playing cards and decided to ambush him while he had the chance. Although he was charged with murder, the trial was deadlocked.

In the months that followed, the body count attributed to this Gospel-blubbering lunatic continued to rise on a pistol-for-hire basis. Incredibly, he even managed a short-lasting stint as a Texas Ranger. On the side, he still ran his more profitable trade as a hired hitman. In 1908, he was strongly suspected as one of the conspirators in the killing of Pat Garrett, although he slickly avoided murder charges.

While a confirmed number of kills may never be known, some rank him as the all-time deadliest of western gunmen, with an estimated 40 or more victims dying by his accord.

In 1909, Deacon Jim was contracted to murder a lawman

named Gus Bobbitt. The killer-for-hire gleefully ambushed his target, but didn't wound him badly enough to bring instant death. The dying Bobbitt lived long enough to offer a description of the clothes his attacker was wearing and the horse he rode out on. This information eventually led to Miller's capture.

A smooth-talking individual who was skilled at conning his way out of tough situations, Deacon Jim bragged he would escape the death sentence and possibly even conviction, with his auditory skills, aided by a high-priced lawyer. Citizens left indignant from the shock effects of the crime felt otherwise, but decided to take no chances.

On April 19, a band of vigilantes broke Miller and three accomplices out of jail in Ada, Oklahoma, hanging them in a barn.

TOM MIX

(1881 - 1940)
Film Star /
Wild West Show Star

Tom Mix *(Photo: Hollywood Book and Poster Shop)*

Born Mix Ron in Pennsylvania, this unusual character would later change his name to Tom Mix and become a hero the world would idolize, as the Wild West was drawing to a close.

For a short time, Mix contributed much to the myth surrounding the gunfighters, lawmen, and sharpshooters of the past, beginning in 1902, when he first found interest in this field. A member of the Oklahoma Cavalry Band, while living in Guthrie, then later a member of Bullock's Cowboy Brigade, he took to the spotlight with fervor and saw a potential, profitable career breaking out.

He made his first film in 1909, while working for Widerman's Wild West Show that same year. This launched a number of other projects, including more movies, personal appearances, and traveling tours, which made him the most popular cowboy in America. In 1911, to top it all off, he served as temporary town marshal of Dewey, Oklahoma.

Mix's film credits were numerous, including "The Rainbow Trail," "The Lone Star Ranger," "Sky High," and "The Fighting Streak." Heading a Wild West extravaganza, he also toured Canada and Europe for live appearances, increasing his popularity.

Scandals, though, were nothing new to this often-married, hard-drinking entertainer, who was not as cleancut in real life as the screen image he portrayed. He was killed in a car crash in 1940 along the old Tucson Highway.

A monument marking the spot where he died was erected and has been routinely vandalized for the last few decades.

BENJAMIN MOEUR

(1869 - 1937)
Doctor / Politician

Born in Texas, Dr. Benjamin Moeur relocated in Arizona, where he set up a medical office in Tempe.

The labors of a frontier doctor were his while the West was still wild, but as changing times came, he sought to change careers, entering the world of politics.

By the time Moeur reached the governor's office, serving from 1933 to 1937, as a Democrat, the West had already changed. The rustlers and gunfighters of the past now drove cars instead of relying on horses, wore double-breasted suits instead of Levis, and found the tommygun more practical than the Colt 45, like their gangster counterparts in the East.

Moeur, however, remained a throwback to earlier times, displaying a practical frontier logic that endeared him to many. The governor cut various taxes, but saw to it that luxury items were taxed, which made him liked by the general population, but hated by gigantic businesses, who in part, developed a mud-slinging smear-campaign that kept him from retaining office. He lost the next primary election.

The positive contributions given to Arizona by this foul-mouthed, western wildman, were many, regardless of statements to the contrary made by his enemies. While holding his office, he turned the rotunda of the capitol into a medical clinic, in which he treated impoverished citizens during his lunch hour. Other benevolent deeds for the people likewise ensured his spot in history.

A curious sidenote to the doctor-turned politician's life is the fact that during his lifetime, he claimed to have delivered somewhere between 10,000 and 11,000 babies.

BURTON MOSSMAN

(1867 - 1956)
Arizona Ranger

Born in Illinois and raised in Minnesota, Burton Mossman seemed an unlikely candidate to make a name for himself in western lore, yet he did just that.

Heading for New Mexico, he saw work as a cowhand, before drifting into Arizona to carry on his duties as manager for the Aztec Land & Cattle Company. He had several run-ins with rustlers prior to 1900, when his employers went out of business, leaving him out of a job.

He spent a short time as a meatcutter, then applied for an interview for a government position related to crime prevention. This action changed his destiny, as he was assigned to lead a 12-man outfit to be called the Arizona Rangers.

Fighting lawbreakers was a task he took to with almost uncanny enthusiasm, chasing down several different wanted men, some of whom were brought back alive, others draped across a saddle.

The murderer, Juan Saliveras, was one of the less fortunate, shot down by Mossman in a face-to-face gunfight, while the elusive Augustine Chacon proved to be far more difficult a prey to track. Devoting much time to his capture, the head Ranger was able to snag the diminutive bad man only days before resigning from his position in order to follow a political career, directed to safer, administrative work within the government.

He died in Roswell, New Mexico, on September 5, 1956, confined to a wheelchair during the last years of his life. He survived his arch-enemy, Chacon, who was hanged in 1902, by over five decades.

SYLVESTER MOWRY

(18?? - 1871)
Soldier / Businessman

An outspoken, flamboyant man, Sylvester Mowry was sent to Arizona from Salt Lake City in 1855 after angering Brigham Young by having an affair with one of the daughters-in-law of the Mormon kingpin.

Afterward, he started a mining business in the Patagonia area and became quite wealthy. He was also well-liked by a number of people who voted this former army officer as a delegate to Congress in 1860, but since there was no official Arizona Territory at the time, he wasn't seated.

This so infuriated the would-be politician, he launched a savage campaign to see his area receive territorial status, growing so caught up in the madness, he offended a newspaper editor named Ed Cross. After an exchange of insults, they agreed to fight a duel, a showdown with rifles as the chosen weapon. This battle was held, with laughable results, as both men missed, shrugged things off, and proceeded to get drunk together.

As the Civil War reached Arizona this controversial character encountered serious political problems. Arrested and sent to Fort Yuma as a Confederate spy, these charges were never proven and little became of them. While held captive, however, his mines were plundered, leaving him more irate and a good deal poorer than ever. He tried suing several parties for damages, but died before collecting compensation.

The last years of his life were reportedly spent in utter, perhaps justifiable bitterness, as he tried to restore both his family honor and his fortune.

WILLIAM MULDOON
Wrestler / Promoter

William Muldoon
dressed for a
theatrical role.
*(Photo from the
collection of
Charles E.
Gilbert)*

During the 1880's, William Muldoon or "Big Bill" as he was sometimes called, brought pro wrestling to the West via a sweeping tour which emphasized Texas as a place of profit.

The authenticity of such shows might have been suspect on some occasions, but other incidents indicate his wrestlers fought tooth-and-nail, in what amounted to little more than bare-knuckle brawling, under the guise of sport.

Muldoon reportedly encouraged those in his employment not to follow the rules, but to break or at least bend them when the situation called for it or if the audience looked bored. Thus, the action got fairly wild, with winners receiving a higher purse than losers, further incentive to make combatants go for the victory, rather than the glory or the old cliche of, "it's not whether you win or lose, but how fairly you play the game."

Another, more dubious charge exists concerning Muldoon's capers, including a carnivalish scam which fixed the ends of certain matches in accordance with side bets being made. One of the oldest tricks in the book, the participants would go opposite the odds, stage an "upset" victory and split the profit from within. Other shady tricks likewise abound concerning Muldoon and a dozen others like him.

Was he for real or was he a faker? This question remained as big a mystery back then as the present mystery concerning modern, big time wrestling. Were the bouts staged, real, or a little bit of both?

While various espose material has placed much infamy on the modern pro circuit, the doings of Muldoon's time, as they actually were, may never be known.

JOAQUIN MURIETA

(1832 - 1853 ?)
Outlaw

Called "The Ghost Of Sonora" and other romantic nicknames, Joaquin Murieta's history remains clouded in an unseparable mingling of fact and fiction.

Supposedly a ranch hand in Stockton, California, he took to robbing and plundering with the charisma of a western Robin Hood. Whether he was good or bad depended on the viewpoint, as white settlers, ranchers, and miners loathed him like smallpox or cholera, while the Mexican population, feeling oppressed, saw him as a champion for justice.

In the beginning he worked alone, but eventually built up a legion of helpers, operating from the Sonora, California homebase, hence his alias. By early 1853, he and his raiders were the most feared riders in the area, with gossip far overshadowing their true-to-life exploits.

While Murieta was credited with the killing of over 100 men, modern-day historians see this as a stretched-out figure, far higher than his probable, truthful total, which remains unknown, but was assuredly much less. How much wealth he may have assembled likewise remains suspect, although treasure hunters still search for lost riches hidden by his band, to this very day.

Even Murieta's death remains questionable. In late 1853, he was supposedly captured and decapitated, with the head going on exhibit afterward. The raids, however, continued for a long time to come, leaving it suspect whether the outlaw had been executed after all or if someone else had died in his place by mistake.

NANA

(1815 - 1895)
Indian leader

One of the numerous leaders among the Chiricahua Apaches, in the same category as Loco, Victorio, and Geronimo, his compatriots in terrorism.

Constantly escaping from the reservation lands, he provided many trials for U.S. and Mexican armies alike, as well as any non-Apache unlucky enough to cross his path. He was a skilled technician and evasive as the wind, sometimes eluding the pursuit of literally thousands of soldiers out to capture or kill him.

When Victorio met death in 1880, following a confrontation with troops, Nana took over as leader of the renegade Chiricahuas. Although aged and partially crippled from the effects of numerous wounds received in countless battles, he began a reign of terror which lasted some six years, using Victorio as an inspiration for savaging both the Mexican and white population.

He raided, he stole, he burned. and always managed to outwit his enemies. A surrender to General George Crook in 1883 and confinement to the San Carlos Reservation proved to be short-lived, as he broke out with Geronimo shortly afterward and continued his rampage, an amazing accomplishment for a man in his late 60's.

This time, however, his vendetta was met with more heavy resistance. In 1886, things came to a close when he was recaptured for the final time.

Sent to Fort Sill, Oklahoma, Nana spent the rest of his days old and infirm, dreaming about the glories of the past. He died at the age of 80, perhaps still plotting somewhere in the back of his mind, a way to escape into the open range once again.

BUCKEY O'NEILL

(1860 - 1898)
Lawman / Rough Rider

Born as William O'Neill, he was nicknamed "Buckey" because of his habit of "bucking the tiger" at faro tables, and not because of his horsemanship or lack of it, as some mistakenly believe.

Originally a newspaper editor, he later took to law, becoming one of the few Arizona-based "gunfighters" who never killed anyone in a showdown. He had his shootouts, to be

Buckey O'Neill *(Photo: Sharlot Hall Museum Library and Archives)*

certain, as in Phoenix when he and fellow lawman, Henry Garfias, did battle with some unruly cowboys. Garfias shot to kill, but O'Neill shot to subdue.

Later, when a gang of bandits held up the Atlantic & Pacific Express near Flagstaff, on the night of March 20, 1889, he chased the crooks for over 600 miles, catching three of them after another non-fatal exchange of lead.

In 1897, he was elected to a new profession, mayor of Prescott, but before his term expired, the Spanish-American War broke out. With patriotism burning inside, he left politics for battle. He was shot at the age of 38 on July 1, 1898, just before the Rough Rider attack on San Juan Hill, dying from a sniper's bullet.

For a man of undeniable courage, O'Neill's unusual lack of bloodlust and an ambition to bring in his prey alive is further proven with the Prescott hanging of Dennis Dilda. While watching the execution, brave and dauntless Buckey seemed undisturbed, but as the outlaw was suspended between heaven and earth, O'Neill flinched, then fainted at the sight.

WILLIAM OURY

(1817 - 1887)

Pioneer

Perhaps the busiest and most versatile of Western note-worthies, William Oury served as an explorer, soldier, Texas Ranger, cattle baron, politician, Indian fighter, newspaper editor, and businessman.

He also might be included in the gunfighter category, with two dead men to his credit, via duels. The surprising thing is, had he not been selected to go for help rather than stay behind, he never would have lived to do these various things, for he was one of the volunteers at The Alamo, missing the massacre when sent by William Travis to Gonzalez, Texas as a courier.

While he avoided an unpleasant fate this way, any charges of cowardice were quickly disproven, as he resumed fighting in the Mexican-American War.

While riding for the Overland Stage, Oury settled in Arizona, starting up a newspaper as well. He became the first mayor of Tucson in 1864, but by no means retired to a peaceful existence, engaging head-first in numerous conflicts with the Apaches. As a rancher, he likewise gained fame for his introduction of short-horned cattle to the area and various experiments in upgrading poor-quality Spanish stock.

In his last years of life, Oury took on yet another activity as a director of the Arizona Pioneers' Historical Society which was based in Tucson. A younger brother, Granville, likewise kept active in Southwestern business and politics.

PERRY OWENS

(1852 - 1919)
Lawman

Born in Tennessee, this colorful character migrated west as a buffalo hunter, ranch hand, and gunfighter.

In November of 1886, he was elected sheriff of Apache County, Arizona, on a campaign promise to end rustler domination and corruption within the law-enforcement office, which, prior to his coming, had been rampant. He quickly set out to make good his vow, killing Ike Clanton and bringing his brother Phineas to justice, then shooting a rustler named Mart Blevins.

Shortly afterward, he went to Holbrook, where in a spectacular gun battle, he killed two more of the Blevins clan, after they resisted arrest, along with another outlaw named Moses Roberts. His elaborate career was tainted somewhat by his involvement in the ugly Pleasant Valley War, but he remained a respected and flashy character throughout his legal career, certainly demonstrating more integrity than a number of lawmen who had come before him.

On December 31, 1888 he turned in his badge, married Elizabeth Barrett in 1902, invested in a store, and died peacefully in Seligman, Arizona, on May 10, 1919.

Aside from his reputation as a brave fighter and deadly shot, Owens tended to be quite theatrical, most likely patterning himself after Bill Cody and Wild Bill Hickok. He liked to wear his hair long, at times almost waist length, wear fancy clothes, and wide-brimmed hats with a multitude of decorative bands.

While he looked like some foppish dandy or stage actor, his appearance was certainly deceptive and no one ever laughed at him to his face.

ALFRED PACKER

(1858 - 1915)
Prospector / Guide / Killer

Alfred Packer made history when in the fall of 1883, he was hired to lead five men from Colorado into New Mexico.

In the midst of their trek, snow set in, leaving them stranded. Eventually their guide left the mountains alone, with no sign of the party that employed him.

An investigation was conducted, leading to a camp they'd made after being unexpectedly trapped by the weather. All that remained of the five members of ths party were butchered remains. After his arrest, Packer admitted he had eaten parts of these men in order to survive, remarking emphatically how the taste wasn't bad if he could keep his mind off the nature of his meals.

He denied, however, having killed anyone, claiming another member of the band, known to him only as Bell, had been the one to slaughter the rest of the party. Packer claimed this man tried to kill him as well, but was fought off and wound up on the receiving, rather than the giving, end of death.

Since the rest of the victims were lifeless, a stewpot was boiling, and Bell had already begun to cook the remains. He felt there was no point in starving to death. Packer figured he would simply finish what another person had begun. The law didn't see things that way, believing he had, in fact, killed and eaten the other members of his group.

Packer was jailed, escaped, and picked up again, this time sentenced to death, but a new trial brought him a 40-year term instead. He was released from the Canon City penitentiary in 1910 and died of natural causes in 1915, still insisting he had murdered no one, but only eaten the remains of another man's handiwork.

TOMAS PARRONDO

(1857 - 1900)
Bullfighter

Tomas Parrondo prior to a bull-fight. *(Photo from the author's collection)*

Born in Madrid, Tomas Parrondo was a reputable matador who scored some noteworthy triumphs in his native land, but held a lifelong ambition to visit Latin America.

It was this decision that writers from his time period mistakenly attributed as a cause for his death, where modern knowledge assumes he would have died anyway, regardless of where he went. For a time though, this dare-devil Spaniard was one of the Wild West's most beloved bullfighters and recognized as a drawing card by numerous promoters.

His first voyage to Mexico was originally intended to be short-term, beginning 1887, but he stayed two years, returning to Spain in late 1889 only after being offered a career-enhancing fight in Barcelona. Shortly afterward, he returned to Mexico, stopping in Cuba along the way, where he remained until the mid-1890's. His final return to Iberia was marked with much tragedy and speculation.

Writers from his time invariably commented that he "contracted a cruel mental illness while in Mexico," which caused him to lose his memory, act irrationally, and ramble on about things which made no sense. Unable to continue his trade, he died mysteriously and mad, on April 15, 1900.

Keeping in mind that in this era many still believed mental problems to be caused by physical means which could be contracted like a cold or smallpox, one could see how germs supposedly picked up during his travels were blamed for his downfall.

In viewing the symptoms more closely and from a modern view, it seems more likely the man died from a brain tumor, undiagnosable and untreatable at the time.

CHARLIE PIERCE

(1850's? - 1895)
Outlaw

Claiming to come from Painted Rock, Texas, Charlie (sometimes spelled Charley) Pierce rode with the Daltons and later, alongside Bill Doolin, but was far more clever than many bandit counterparts.

While robbing and blasting his way through numerous illegal activities, he maintained a legitimate counter-image that lasted for a long while, as a racehorse owner in Pawnee, Oklahoma. Eventually, though, the veil fell down and the dark-haired, moustached gentleman-by-day, robber-by-night was discovered for what he really was.

In June of 1895, Pierce robbed an express office in Woodward, alongside his friend, fellow outlaw Bittercreek George Newcome. The duo hid out at the ranch of some other affiliates, the Dunns, lying low while the reward for them climbed over $5,000 apiece.

A month later, the bloody finale came for both, although accounts vary as to exactly what happened. Their hideout discovered by some farmers, Pierce and Newcome were gunned down, the former taking so many bullet wounds, writers at the time commented on how he resembled a human lead mine. The dramatic version states the two men saw riders coming and opened fire, coming out second best in the gunfight, but other, less glorious accounts indicate the two may have been found asleep and ambushed in effective, but bloody form.

This argument might be substantiated by the fact that Pierce had bullet wounds in the soles of his feet, hardly the injuries received by a man standing his ground a la Custer vs. Indians and fighting to the death.

ALBERT PIKE

(1809 - 1891)
Educator / Author / Philosopher

Born in Boston on December 29, 1809, Albert Pike spent much of his life moving about the South, Midlands, and West, as he plied various trades including teacher, newspaperman, and soldier.

In 1846, he obtained the rank of captain in the army, seeing action in the war with Mexico over the Texas territory. It was in the world of Freemasonry, however, that he became an important and respected figurehead.

Joining the Western Star Masonic Lodge in Little Rock, Arkansas, he later became the first Worshipful Master of the newly chartered Magnolia Lodge in that same city. He advanced into the Scottish Rite as well, where in 1859, he was elected Sovereign Grand Commander of the Supreme Grand Council in this extension of Masonry, holding the position for over three decades.

He continued to write, lecture, and devote time to the fraternity for the rest of his life. He died on April 2, 1891, at the age of 81, having lost the ability to speak and writing his last words on a piece of paper. Three times, he scrawled out Shalom, meaning peace.

Pike's concepts and writings proved valuable to the spread of Masonry, which was growing rapidly in the West, boasting such members over the years as Pat Garrett, Bill Cody, and a host of others. One of the most articulate and educated men of his time, he not only studied and philosophized upon concepts of Freemasonry, but became an expert in linguistics, speaking ancient Persian, Aryan, Hebrew, Sumerian, Chaldean, Greek and Latin, as well as various American Indian languages.

While over 70 years old, he became the first man to translate the Veda, the source of philosophy for the Hindu religion, into English.

ZEBULON PIKE

(1779 - 1813)
Explorer

Born in New Jersey, Zebulon Pike started off as a soldier while still in his teens and from that point onward, tended to live a spiced-up, adventuresome life.

He became an explorer, specializing in the use of the keelboat, and studied the various rivers of America. He made friends of some Indian tribes, foes of others, documented his discoveries to the best of his capabilities, and mapped out the routes he took for future use.

In 1806, he set out on yet another lengthy expedition, which led him into Colorado and there, he discovered what would later be called Pike's Peak. Braving the winter, he and his crew drifted downward into Mexico, marched through Chihuahua, and back up to Louisiana, where the ordeal ended.

Pike published his findings during this aforementioned exploration, through the old C & A Conrad Company in Philadelphia. These were later resold into numerous foreign translations. These writings gained him more fame than money and, while respected at the time, were later proven to contain a number of inaccuracies.

Rather than further exploring, he was content to rest upon his laurels, but the unexpected War of 1812 changed these plans. Given the rank of brigadier general, he was killed in 1813, while fighting in Toronto against the British forces.

Pike's Peak, however, remains behind as one of Colorado's key tourist attractions, although the explorer most surely discovered it by sheer chance.

JOHN RINGO

(1850 ? - 1882)
Outlaw / Cowboy / Drunkard

Movies such as "$100,00 For Ringo," "A Pistol For Ringo," "The Return of Ringo," "Ringo & His Golden Pistol," plus countless others and the famous song from the 1960's have nothing in common with the real John Ringo but his name.

In truth, Ringo was not the desperately-hunted bandit that myth later made him to be. He was not a gunfighter either, nor was he a particularly flamboyant personality, although seemingly well-read and educated beyond most others in Tombstone, Arizona, where he roamed.

While he liked to recite poetry and biblical quotations, his real love was for alcohol, which stirred his radical mood swings that borderlined on manic-depressive. This supposed gunfighter spoke more on the desire to shoot himself than others, especially when full of liquor.

There were times when he would ride off for days in order to be alone, with fellow Clanton Ranch employees worrying about his safety. Far from the dashing pistolero of legend, he was a sullen, brooding man with deep emotional problems.

He was also a man of mystery, never photographed and with few people knowing his real name. Some historians cite this as John Ringold, others know him as John Ringould.

Only one proven death remains attributed to this man, when he grew annoyed with an unidentified drunk who kept making remarks about a prostitute who was trying to ply her trade. In a fit of drunken rage, Ringo sought to defend the soiled dove's honor by bashing the man across the head with his revolver, then shooting him in the throat. So much for being a big-time gunman.

While it was never proven, Ringo supposedly took part in the ambushes against Morgan and Virgil Earp, shooting not face-to-face as the gunfighter myths would claim, but hidden in darkness, along with a group of friends. Suspicion remains easily directed his way, for he was an avowed hater of both the Earp clan and their friend Doc Holliday. He had also reportedly lamented missing out on the OK Corral gun battle.

In the early summer of 1882, Ringo was found dead, propped against an old tree. In his hand was a gun, in his head was a hole between the right eye and ear. While many people would later claim to be his killer, including Buckskin Frank Leslie, whom he'd been drinking with the night before, and Wyatt Earp, who was among other things, a teller of tall tales, evidence most likely points to the fact that finally, in a fit of drunken depression, Ringo decided to make good his numerous threats about self-destruction.

Ringo's grave is not among his cohorts in Tombstone's Boot Hill, but may be found by taking Highway 181 south outside of this city, until the road makes a sharp turn at Turkey Creek. Instead of turning east, the interested party should turn west on a dirt road running south of Turkey Creek for about ¼ mile. When the traveler reaches a farmhouse on the north side of the road, there stands a fenced-off area, which contains Ringo's headstone and a historical plaque.

The hard-drinking, Shakespeare-quoting ranch hand whom history has mistakenly converted from a petty outlaw into the most feared gunman who ever walked the West, rests peacefully in the ground, below the shade of the very same tree his body was discovered slumped against at the time of his death.

While Tombstone attracts all the tourists, little mention is ever made of this added, nearby attraction. Alone in death, as he was in life, the late John Ringo probably wouldn't have minded that at all.

FELIX ROBERT

(1862 - 1916)
Bullfighter / Promoter
Rodeo Figurehead

Felix Robert *(Photo from the author's collection)*

Born Pierre Cazenave in Meilhan, France, his first profession in a long and unusual life was that of waiter in a cafe in Mont de Marsan.

Deciding he wanted more adventure out of life, he moved to Seville, Spain, where he studied bullfighting under the tutoring of the celebrated matador, Manuel Carmona. From 1894 to 1899, he gave the public several fine afternoons, adding to his fame by an interesting publicity stunt, the addition of a mustache, something only one other man had worn prior to that date, in over 250 years of organized bullfighting. In 1900, he made a move to Mexico, where once again, his career took a dramatic turn.

Settling in Ciudad Juarez, across from wild El Paso, he quickly saw the bullfight as a great moneymaker, if it could be distorted to fit the cowboy interest in the U.S.A. Thus he rented the local bullring, promoting not only standard bullfights, but every type of entertainment he could think of.

Knowing the Americans liked rodeos, he combined certain elements from this world with the bullfight he already knew and while the result resembled little more than a circus sideshow, crowds at the stadium doubled. Among the shows Robert organized were contests between fighting bulls and bears or mountain lions, with betting on the side, trick riding exhibitions, and the addition of various comedy acts.

The business boom might have lasted the rest of his life, had it not been for the political stormclouds brewing at the time. In anticipation of the Revolution, he decided to go back to France, dying in Marseille on January 19, 1916, from natural causes.

GEORGE RUFFNER

(1862 ? - 1933)

Lawman

At the time of his death, George Ruffner was the oldest Arizona sheriff in both age and seniority, climaxing a lifelong career which, among other things, won him a spot in the National Cowboy Hall of Fame in Oklahoma City.

Quick with a gun, fast with his wits, and a good deal more compassionate than other supposed upholders of law and order during his era, he stood out as what could have easily been the "good guy" role model for a Western film.

Ruffner was best known for the sad duty of having to track down and bring to justice a former friend named Fleming Parker, who had taken to train robbery, jailbreak, and murder. Wanted in particular for the killing of a deputy district attorney named Lee Norris, the badman fled, until he was captured by Ruffner near Flagstaff.

The cunning lawman had reversed the horseshoes on his horse, deceiving the outlaw, who kept checking for tracks to see if he was being trailed and mistakenly assumed the prints were from a rider going in the opposite direction, thus of no concern to him. How wrong he was.

After taking the prisoner back to Prescott, Ruffner held off an angry lynch mob with a shotgun. When the outlaw was legally hanged, Ruffner showed further good spirit, allowing the condemned a final visit from Flossie, one of the prostitutes from nearby Whiskey Row.

While lacking the frills of Perry Owens, the press of Pat Garrett, or the mythological aura of Wyatt Earp, Ruffner was undoubtedly one of the West's most dedicated lawmen.

RUSSIAN BILL

(18?? - 1881)
Outlaw

Born in Russia, William Tattenbaum (most likely an alias he adopted) migrated to the United States in 1880, deserting the Russian military to avoid a court-martial for punching out a superior officer.

After a brief time spent in California, he migrated to Arizona where he saw employment on the Clanton Ranch. Perhaps disappointed at not being allowed to partake in the outlaw gang's more severe criminal activities, he left for New Mexico, which proved to be a fatal decision on his part.

Making the mistake of stealing a horse, he failed to realize this neck of the woods was less tolerant of scofflaws than Arizona. He was picked up in the tiny town of Shakespeare and tossed into jail, figuring he could either escape or get off with a light sentence when his trial came.

He was surprised to learn his "day in court" was little more than a vigilante hearing, after which he and another bandit named Sandy King were escorted to the banquet hall of the Grant House Hotel, where they were hanged from the rafters, presumedly because there were no trees or poles nearby high enough to do the trick. When his mother, a wealthy Russian countess, made inquiries about what had happened, she was told her son had met an "accidental death" and was buried in Shakespeare.

The town has long since been deserted, with only ruins remaining. The graveyard, where Russian Bill and Sandy King were laid to rest, bore their headstones for several decades, but these, too, have since become lost.

ED SCHIEFFELIN

(1848 - 1898)
Prospector / Miner

Born in Pittsburg, Pennsylvania, Ed Schieffelin dedicated his life to the search for riches, panning and digging throughout the West as he hunted down valuable minerals.

Oregon, Colorado, California, and New Mexico were some of the areas he roamed, prior to his arrival in southern Arizona. In 1877, he announced plans to look for gold and silver in the Dragoon Mountains, to which a friend supposedly remarked, "All you'll find out there is your tombstone!"

Paying no heed, he carried through with his plans and found silver. Remembering what was said earlier, he named the strike "Tombstone" and continued to mine. Tombstone, of course, became the name of the town that was soon to follow.

For a long while, Schieffelin enjoyed a life of high-class living, but eventually returned to prospecting again. In 1898, he was finding silver, but was bitter about the fact that gold eluded him. A few months later, his dead body was discovered just south of Rosenburg. What presumedly killed him was heart failure, due to excitement over finally striking gold ore.

The Schieffelin Monument does not exist in Boot Hill, but is by itself a short distance west of the city limits, signs near the old court house pointng the way for any interested party.

Incidentally, other silver strikes this fortunate miner made included the Graveyard, the Lucky Cuss, and the Tough Nut, the last of which was a name adopted for one of Tombstone's main streets.

JOHN SELMAN

(1839 - 1896)
Outlaw / Gunfighter / Lawman

John Selman, like many of the characters who made up the Wild West, worked for both sides of the law, breaking it in one area and upholding it in another.

Originally from Arkansas, he spent some time in Texas, then headed for New Mexico, where he was part of a bandit gang dubbed Selman's Scouts. He proved to be a rather poor criminal, captured in 1880 after being weakened by a near-fatal case of smallpox. Sent back to Texas where he was wanted for more serious crimes, he spent time in jail, then settled in El Paso, where, ironically, he served as both a deputy sheriff and constable.

Selman remains known for two major killings, the first being Bass Outlaw, a former Texas Ranger turned bad, the second being the infamous John Wesley Hardin. While the general public accepted the former's death, they were not so inclined with the latter.

Since he'd taken the liberty of shooting Hardin in the back as he polished off drinks in the Acme Saloon, a murder charge was filed, which resulted in a hung jury. A second trial was set but never came about because Selman died from gunshot wounds following an argument with another lawman, George Scarborough.

In justifying the killing, Scarborough used the same logic as Selman when explaining why he'd shot Hardin. Selman supposedly threatened to kill him, for some unexplained reason, just as Hardin had earlier boasted about his intention to kill the man who would eventually be his assassin. Thus, he wound up eating lead.

It's a curious chain of events, with Hardin threatening to shoot Selman, then being killed by him, Selman threatening to kill Scarborough then dying in kind, and this man dying under gunfire a short time later.

LUKE SHORT

(1854 - 1893)

Gambler / Gunfighter

Although born in Mississippi, Luke Short grew up in Texas, running away while still a teenager, in order to join a trail drive.

It was in this environment he learned to deal cards and play other games of chance, via the cowboys he worked with. Soon, he was better at gambling than range work and realized he had a new calling in life. As a hustler, his skills were undeniable, but as a gunfighter, his accomplishments have been vastly overrated.

After some time spent in Nebraska, he showed up in Arizona, where in Tombstone he killed a drunkard named Charlie Storms on February 25, 1881. With this action deemed justifiable, no charges were placed against him, but he decided it best to move on. He settled in Kansas, then headed for Texas when the gambling turned cold.

In Fort Worth, he ran into Jim Courtright, who tried to hit him up for protection money in regard to the saloon he had purchased. When Short refused to pay and evicted the long-haired extortionist from his property, tempers flared. On February 8, 1887, the bitterness between the two men erupted in gunplay. Short luckily wounded his opponent with the first shot, blowing off his thumb and thus making it easy to empty the revolver into him without fear of being fired back upon. Short was the winner, but his days, too, were numbered.

On September 8, 1893, the legendary gambler/gunman passed away from dropsy. His wild lifestyle, excessive drinking, and poor health habits added up on him and these were odds he couldn't beat. Knowing he was going to die, he purchased his own headstone in advance and bought the graveplot at Fort Worth's Oakwood Cemetery, where he was laid to rest.

AL SIEBER

(1844 - 1907)
Indian Fighter / Scout / Lawman

Born in Germany, Al Sieber drifted west following the Civil War. A wound he took in the leg at Gettysburg left him a gimping half-cripple.

He took up work in Arizona as a scout for the various cavalry units and got tangled up in the Indian conflicts, particularly after one of his assistants, a shadowy character referred to in history as The Apache Kid, shot him in his already-mangled leg.

With Geronimo's surrender in 1886, this period in Sieber's life came to an end and he found a new job as a deputy U.S. marshal. This kept him busy for a time, then his career changed again as he became foreman over various workers assigned to build Roosevelt Dam. It was while carrying out these duties, he met with destiny.

On February 19, 1907, Sieber was killed when a premature explosion started a rock slide, which crushed him to death.

An interesting side-note about this man involves his training of the young Tom Horn, who worked with him as a scout and absorbed considerable knowledge about life in the wilderness. Unlike Sieber, Horn used his experience for evil rather than good, eventually becoming a hired killer and dying on the gallows.

JOHN SLAUGHTER

(1841 - 1922)

Lawman

Born in Louisiana, but raised in Texas, this interesting little man stood only 5' 3", but carried a big gun and an even bigger reputation.

First a soldier, then a Texas Ranger, he later took to wearing a sheriff's badge, once he relocated in Arizona. He, and not Wyatt Earp, might best be credited for cleaning up Tombstone, as he introduced a "be gone or be shot" policy which caused remaining rulebreakers who had not been jailed or gunned down in the early 1880's to take notice.

When scoffers failed to listen, the little gunfighter was quick to back up his promises. Guadalupe Robles and an associate named Deron found this out following a train robbery near Nogales in 1888, when Slaughter tracked them down. Refusing to surrender when given the chance proved a fatal mistake. They left the Whetstone Mountains as a pair of corpses.

Likewise was the probable fate of a bandit named Juan Soto, who "disappeared" after incurring Slaughter's wrath and most assuredly met an unpleasant, though unproven end at the hands of the "Little Giant" of law-enforcement officials. An elusive killer named Chacon proved more trying, however, with Slaughter having him cornered and for one of the few times in his life, missing with his gun and enabling the outlaw to escape.

In 1891, figuring it was time to retire, before another such flaw in aim proved fatal, he switched to ranching and lived into his 80's. He died on December 15, 1922, from natural causes.

JOHN SONTAG

(1860 - 1893)

Outlaw

Along with his brother, George, and a bandit named Christopher Evans, John Sontag took to a short-lived life of crime when a quartz mine he owned at Visalia, California failed to produce the riches he desired.

The efforts of this would-be gang were more or less bungled, with George being sent to prison following a train robbery in Fresno County. Blaming the Pinkertons for his brother's arrest, John declared war on all lawmen, but especially representatives of this celebrated detective agency. He and Evans took to stopping stagecoaches several times, not to rob them, as much as to search for Pinkerton workers on board, which became a fixation to both men.

In 1893, the law closed in on Sontag's hideout in Visalia, shooting it out in an eight hour gunbattle. In the process, two deputy sheriffs from Tulare County were killed, with Evans and Sontag both badly wounded. The former, who denied ever having taken part in robberies with the two brothers at any point in time (although stolen loot was found on his farm), lost an eye in the gunfight. He was sent to jail, escaped, was captured, and re-imprisoned until 1911.

Sontag, however, died a short time after the shootout ended, his injuries far more critical than those of his partner. Evans, incidentally, moved to Oregon after his release from prison and died in Portland from natural causes in 1917.

Based mainly on the merit of his final confrontation with the law, John Sontag was branded a cold-blooded, ruthless criminal, when in truth, his actions were petty, poorly-planned and, finally, self-destructive.

BELLE STARR

(1848 - 1889)

Outlaw

Born in Carthage, Missouri, on February 5, 1848, Myra Belle Shirley grew up to become Belle Starr, the most well-known female bandit in American history.

Dubbed with such seductive nicknames as "The Pearl of the Wild West" and "The Bandit Queen" by the media, she scared more men with her looks than with her guns, if the truth ever managed to surface. A beauty queen she wasn't and if Helen of Troy had a face beautiful enough to launch a thousand ships, Belle had a face that could sink them.

Her exploits, like her nonexistent beauty, were vastly overblown. She was no more a Lady Robin Hood than she was a glamour girl, as a closer examination of her records show.

In 1866 she was seduced by Cole Younger and gave birth to an illegitimate daughter, as Younger had decided it best to head back to Missouri rather than hang around in Texas, where the Shirley family had taken up residence. Shrugging him off, Belle's attention fell upon a petty crook named Jim Reed, and together they formed quite a couple.

Joining a gang led by John Fischer, they took to a life of crime which brought them through several states, including far-away California. In the meantime, the bandit queen gave birth to another child, fathered by Reed, whom she'd married, and the reign of terror continued.

Returning to Texas, she lost her husband to a lawman's bullet, but failed to slow down in the slightest, becoming close to numerous outlaws in the time that followed, including Sam Starr, Jack Spaniard, Blue Duck, Jimmy French and a host of others. Quite frankly, she managed to make the rounds, in-between hold-ups, bootlegging, horse-stealing, and other illegal activities.

Sending her children away in order to better pursue her criminal career, she added prostituting to her credit, along with burglary, and the fencing of stolen goods. Yet another marriage to a man named Jim July further complicated her life, their relationship turning sour in short order. Rumors have it this final husband may have been the one to pull the trigger on his own wife, for fear of what she'd do to him, after questions about his fidelity arose. Such confirmation, however, will never be proven.

Belle Starr was shot in ambush while riding her horse on February 3, 1889, just outside Younger's Bend, Texas. She was buried beneath a fancy tombstone, with an elaborate poem stating, "Shed not for her the bitter tear, nor give the heart to vain regret. 'Tis but the casket that lies here, the gem that filled it sparkles yet."

The media which delighted in writing about the Bandit Queen's adventures loved it, but those who knew the real Myra Belle Shirley probably gagged.

FRANK STILWELL

(1855 - 1882)

Outlaw

Supposedly born in Texas, Frank Stilwell drifted to southeastern Arizona, where he eventually joined the Clanton gang.

Aside from work as a "ranch hand" for this mob, he made added profit as a stagecoach robber, holding up the lines between Bisbee and Tombstone so many times, the drivers recognized his voice behind the mask and accepted his antics as routine. Surprisingly, Stilwell always managed to avoid jail time, perhaps due to the fact he served simultaneously as a deputy sheriff for John Behan in Cochise County.

Even when his mask slipped off during an 1882 holdup, revealing his identity beyond any shadow of a doubt, little was done to stop him. He made a mistake though, when he made the leap from bandit to killer, taking part in the murder of Morgan Earp, which brought the wrath of brother Wyatt down upon his head.

On March 21, 1882, less than three days following the Earp murder, Stilwell was found dead in Tucson, in the Southern Pacific railroad yard. He had been sent by Ike Clanton to wait on the funeral train carrying Morgan's body and there, kill Wyatt Earp as well. While never fully proven, Doc Holliday and Wyatt Earp have been credited with his shooting, filling his body with four rifle shots and two loads of buckshot fired at close range, which all but tore him in half.

A violent end for a violent, unethical, and totally dislikable man.

DALLAS STOUDENMIRE

(1845 - 1882)
Lawman

Although a heavy drinker, Dallas Stoudenmire did his part to combat lawlessness in Texas.

After a stint with the Texas Rangers, he took to wearing a star in El Paso, where he won the respect of many, but gained some avowed enemies as well. His popularity decreased when a poorly-planned shooting incident brought death to two trouble-makers and an innocent bystander. James, Frank, and George Manning, three friends of the dead men, swore they would gain revenge.

In 1882, this trio played a part in the killing of Doc Cummings, Stoudenmire's brother-in-law. Although the victim was the one who supposedly started a fight with Jim Manning, making retaliation a questionable case of self-defense, the tension between the warring families greatly increased. It was a matter of time before a gun battle erupted.

On September 18 of the same year, the dreaded incident happened. An argument led to shooting, in which a previously neutral member of the Manning clan, known by the nickname of "Doc" just like Stoudenmire's dead brother-in-law, took a bullet in the arm. The lawman, however, didn't come off as lucky, as the rest of the Mannings came to the aid of their fallen kinsman, one of them shooting Stoudenmire in the head. The killing was again deemed as self-defense and no charges were filed against any of the participants.

Stoudenmire evidently died broke, with a family left behind as survivors. The El Paso Freemasons provided various finances for his funeral, since the widow was in desolate condition.

EJ SWIFT

(1827 - 1887)
Fireman

Not too much has been recorded about this resident of Tombstone, Arizona, except that he was a family man and well-liked by most people. The way he died was what won him distinction in the history books, because it was so uncanny.

In March of 1887, Smith was confronted by a saloonkeeper named Jerry Barton, who demanded payment for a liquor bill stemming from a party the fire department had arranged. Words turned to blows, with the 60-year-old Swift holding his own, until he was knocked down. Although the winner of the fight, Barton was apprehended and fined $8.00, which he paid on the spot.

From there he sought out Swift and another brawl ensued, this time with fatal results. Swift, who was grabbed by the beard and held by the angry tavern-owner by one hand, and punched violently with the other, slumped senseless into the street, where efforts to revive him failed. A few minutes later he died, with an autopsy showing his neck had been broken in two places.

Swift received an elaborate burial in Boot Hill, but his wife was sick and nearly out of funds. An unorthodox charity event was held to raise money for her, with men gambling for her late husband's possessions, including a fancy watch. As for Barton, little else remains, although he was supposedly sent to prison for a few years, before dropping out of sight.

What the "EJ" portion of Swift's name stood for also faded from memory, although the "J" was said to refer to "James."

JOHN SWILLING

(1830 ? - 1878)
Pioneer / Prospector / Developer

Born in Georgia, John Swilling, commonly known as "Jack" by his friends, came to Arizona at the close of the Civil War.

For a short time, he searched for gold and silver, with only modest results, establishing himself on the Salt River in 1867. The settlement he established was first dubbed Stonewall, but later came to be known by a far more famous name, Phoenix.

Swilling and associates sought to bring water to the desert lands, making farming easier and more profitable. Thus was developed a series of canals and irrigation ditches which served their purpose more effectively than ever dreamed possible. Afterward, "Jack" became known by several other titles, including "The Father of Arizona Waterways."

Sadly, this pioneer and enterprising ex-miner met an ugly end, when a stagecoach was robbed outside Wickenburg in 1878, with two passengers being killed in the process. For some reason, suspicion fell upon Swilling and one of his friends, although both men loudly protested the charges against them.

While awaiting trial, they were confined to the Yuma County jail. Here, as he considered avenues for legal defense, Swilling took sick and died. He was survived by a wife and several children.

Jack Swilling *(Photo: Salt River Project)*

LEE THAYER
Minister

Lee Thayer was no big name in the religious circles of the time, but his determination to set up a church for Baptists in the Buckeye Valley of Arizona showed overwhelming Western spirit and persistence.

Even more curiously, while this pastor worked for the salvation of souls, his brother, the first doctor in this region, worked at the saving of physical life. Thus the Thayers covered both ends.

Formerly preaching revival in a one-room schoolhouse, things changed for Thayer in April of 1903 when a committee was appointed to erect a permanent church building in Buckeye. With land donated by a Mr. & Mrs. Bruner and a Mr. Benson, a loan of $350, and various donations collected, the building became a reality.

The pastor and his wife hauled the lumber from Phoenix in wagons, Rev. Thayer driving one team, Mrs. Thayer driving another. During church construction, the couple lived on the grounds, residing in a tent. The minister likewise helped in the building of the church where he could, while his wife prepared meals for the carpenters, most of whom volunteered their services. Curiously, the cornerstone was laid for this Baptist church with the assistance of a local Methodist and a Mormon.

Thayer's dream became a reality on schedule, the first service being held in November of 1903. On October 16 of that year, just prior to opening, the church was incorporated under the laws of the territory of Arizona. After much toil, the Baptist faithful finally had a lasting basis in the wilds west of Phoenix.

BEN THOMPSON

(1842 - 1884)

Gunfighter / Gambler

Born in England, Ben Thompson migrated to America with his parents in 1849.

Life in the New World proved an interesting experience for this foreigner, who grew up living both for and against the law, depending on the circumstances at the time. A heavy drinker, risk-taking cardcheat, patron of whores, and sharpshooter, he became well-known for his various deeds of misconduct, earning the reputation of a bully.

Among his many jobs were Texas Ranger, strongarm man for the Atchison, Topeka, & Santa Fe railroad, gun-for-hire, and marshal. He left a trail of bodies behind him everywhere he went, but somehow always avoided the gallows. He became a swaggering, ill-mannered alcoholic, growing more violent and overbearing as he aged.

He seemed convinced all those around him either liked him or feared him so much, they dared do nothing to provoke his wrath. This proved to be a fatal overestimation of his own self-importance.

On March 10, 1884, while attending the Vaudeville Variety Theatre in San Antonio, he was accompanied by another gunfighter named John King Fisher. He was spotted by some old enemies, who put nine slugs into him, any one of which would have been sufficient to kill him. Fisher, too, got caught up in the crossfire and fell from multiple, mortal wounds. As he died, however, he and Thompson managed to kill Joe Foster, one of their assailants.

The shootout eventually came to be regarded as one of the bloodiest incidents in the city's history, although warning signs of its coming existed long before the actual event. Thompson was a man who made people hate him, this time fatally.

TIBURCIO VASQUEZ

(1835 - 1875)

Outlaw

Fleeing from the law after a fight at a dance, in which a white sheriff was killed, Tiburcio Vasquez decided to ride the bandit trail.

In short order, he took to every crime he could think of, including horse stealing, cattle rustling, stagecoach robbery, and murder. Because his victims were mainly Anglos, he had the sympathy and support of the Mexican population behind him, which enabled him to evade capture for as long as he did. While regarded as a cold-hearted killer by some, to others he became a dashing figure who stood for social reform rather than crime.

A superior horseman, clever tracker, and outdoorsman who knew the mountains well, he constantly evaded those sent to capture him, surviving by his own cunning and the frequent help of sympathizers who gave him provisions. By 1873, a reward of $3,000 if taken alive and $2,000 if brought back dead was placed on his head, an extremely high amount for the time, indicating just how much he was wanted by the law.

On May 14, 1874, he was finally arrested in Los Angeles and brought to San Jose where he was tried and sentenced to death. During his stay in prison, he received thousands of visitors, many of them women he'd supposedly courted and others who were in love with the legacy, rather than the man.

On March 19, 1875, he was hanged, adding to his legend with his final statement; "A spirit of hatred took possession of me. I had numerous fights in defense of what I believed to be my rights and those of my countrymen. I believed we were being unjustly deprived of the social rights that belonged to us."

The law evidently didn't agree with his method of social reform!

VICTORIO

(1809 - 1880)
Indian leader

One-time leader of the Eastern branch of the Chiricahua Apaches, Victorio proved himself to be a cunning chief, fierce warrior, and savage renegade.

During the 1870's he proved to be a constant trial to both U.S. and Mexican troops, via his raids, ambushes, and refusal to remain on reservation lands. By 1879, operating out of Chihuahua, Mexico, he became the most feared name in the conflicts between Apaches and white men, but time was running out for him.

On October 14, 1880, a combined effort of Mexican and American soldiers, determined to put a stop to his various barbarities, tracked him and his crew to the Tres Castillos mountains across the Mexican border from present-day El Paso, Texas. The Mexicans sent the Americans back at that point and, free from U.S. supervision, killed all but a handful of the Indians.

Victorio was among the victims, but accounts of his death remain speculative. Some claim he was killed by a fellow Indian, a Tarahumara scout who worked for the Mexicans, while others claim, facing certain defeat, the warrior decided to take his own life. The bloody saga did not end here, however, for Nana and other Apaches took up the struggle where Victorio left off, using his death as an inspiration for battle and retaliation.

For over two decades, Victorio was an active raider and strategist, who experts claim possessed one of the greatest military minds among all Indians. Elusive, well-organized, and clever, he constantly proved himself to be the embodiment of a stereotyped Indian warrior.

PANCHO VILLA

(1877 - 1923)
Outlaw / Bandit / Revolutionary

Sources conflict concerning this complex personality, who was part killer, part clown.

Some list his name as Doroteo Arango, while others claim him to be Jose Francisco Villa Arambulla or an assortment of other monickers. Whatever the case, the Mexican Revolution enabled this bank robber, con man, and cattle thief to make an about face and become one of the most colorful characters of the dying West. For most purposes, he could be considered the last of the dashing gunfighters or stereotyped Mexican bandits to roam at large, clearly outliving his times.

When the revolution started, Villa joined Madero against President Diaz. Originally allied with the notorious General Huerta, Villa's victories in battle were well-recognized, although in 1912, his luck ran out for him. Huerta, double-crossing most of his friends, ordered Villa among those arrested, tried and sentenced to the firing squad.

Madero gave him a reprieve, which was scarcely needed, as shortly afterward, the outlaw-turned-pseudo-soldier escaped from jail. In 1913, he resurfaced, siding with Carranza to retaliate against Huerta. Villa, however, proved gullible once more, as this new associate likewise pulled a double-cross and the two forces wound up fighting each other in a series of conflicts spanning spring through fall of 1915.

Humiliated by this and evidently seeing a potential political career go down the drain, Villa pulled an uncanny publicity stunt, raiding the continental United States! This, too, proved to be controversial, making the outlaw a bold and dashing figure to some, to others a grotesque court jester who wore a sombrero rather than a cap with bells.

The raid took place on March 9, 1916, when Villa rode through Columbus, New Mexico, whooping up a storm. The bandit leader chose to attack by day, rather than by night, as would have been more effective, to assure photographers could take his picture during the attack. The result was less than spectacular with dead and wounded on both sides. Villa quickly rode back to Mexico, evading the efforts of General Pershing to catch him.

Pershing, in turn, was denied permission to set up a base in the Mexican interior, occupying the capital of Chihuahua, where Villa liked to operate, feeling certain sooner or later the outlaw would return there. President Wilson, already preoccupied with the war going on in Europe, felt doing so might provoke a war with Mexico as well, which was what he needed least. Villa, more cunning than many gave him credit for, may have counted on this reaction from the President to begin with, which prompted him to pull off the raid which made him a dubious celebrity.

Through 1920, Villa continued to ride, but his actions were outright banditry. He also took the liberty of marrying several widows in different locations, handily created for the taking by the revolution. Finally, an interim President De La Huerta literally bribed the outlaw to retire from activity, which he did.

His quiet time was short-lived, for on July 20, 1923, the Villa legacy came to a bloody conclusion in Parral, Mexico. There, he and others riding in an automobile, were massacred in a hail of gunshots.

Pancho Villa *(Photo: New Mexico State Records Center and Archives)*

TOM WATERS

(1840 ? - 1881)
Prospector

A powerfully-built, heavy-drinking man, Tom Waters came into Tombstone with some money in his pocket in July of 1881.

In the midst of his drinking, he purchased a black and blue plaid shirt, which he thought was attractive, but all those around him found somewhat silly-looking on a person of his size. Tired of the wisecracks and growing more irritable as he drank, he vowed to punch out the next person to make fun of his new piece of clothing. Sure enough, a friend named Bradshaw made some commentary on how the shirt resembled a table-cloth, which got him knocked out for his honesty.

When he revived, Bradshaw was furious, not only because his supposed-friend had hit him over a remark made in jest, but because he'd been injured by the blow, a cut open over one eye. Going home, he patched himself up, got his gun, and went to settle the score.

Waters, in the meantime, had gone to another saloon, punched another man for laughing at the shirt, then moved onward. As Waters continued his drinking spree, Bradshaw approached, asked, "Why did you hit me?" and fired four shots before a response was given.

Tom Waters died a few minutes after being wounded, shot once in the chest, twice in the shoulder area, and once in the head. His body rests in Boot Hill to this day, perhaps the only man in history ever killed because of the color of a shirt.

CHARLES WEBER

(1813 - 1881)
Pioneer / Colonist / Developer

One of the early-day citizens who saw potential in land-purchase and envisioned the West as a place for opportunity, Charles Weber was one of numerous men to capitalize on California's expansion. Heading to the Northland, he became an investor and builder worthy of note.

Weber purchased 48,747 square acres of ground under the Mexican Land Grant in 1845. Two years later, he had a town site surveyed, which he in turn developed and named Stockton. The city he started was incorporated under the California Constitution in August of 1850, a full month before California itself was granted statehood.

This newly-founded development, which Weber lived to see expand, was located in an area perfect for farming, ranching, and wine-making. Even to this day, Stockton and surrounding cities, which sprang up afterward, remain known for these businesses.

Weber's early-day Stockton eventually drew other settlers, including one Samuel Purdy, who became the town's first mayor, and a number of Portuguese immigrants, who came later on. The area still contains a great many Portuguese-American residents to this very day.

Weber died in 1881, long after first dreaming of, drawing up, and organizing his colony.

THOMAS WHALEY

(1823 - 1890)

Pioneer / Businessman / Ghost

Born in New York on October 5, 1823, Thomas Whaley became one of the early-day settlers to develop southern California.

Arriving in San Francisco in 1849, after a dangerous trip around Cape Horn on the SS Sutton, a voyage which took over 200 days, he quickly found the Northland to his disliking and headed south. In 1851, he established himself in what is present-day "Old Town" in San Diego, went back east to marry in 1853, then returned.

Here he remained with his family until 1873, when he left once more, venturing back for the final time in 1879. He died on December 14, 1890, with his remains being put to rest in San Diego's Mount Hope Cemetery. His spirit, however, did not sleep so quietly.

According to legend, Whaley's ghost still haunts the infamous Whaley House, one of Old Town's prime attractions, still open for tours, along with an assortment of visitors from the Twilight Zone, who have assembled here. This house, completed in 1857, served as not only the home for the Whaley family, but a courthouse as well, as there were no public buildings to accommodate trials at the time.

People have claimed to smell cigar smoke in the air at unexplained times, supposedly without knowing Whaley was a lover of Havanas, while other discontented spirits, including a boat-thief railroaded to a hanging, join him in terrorizing the room where court was once held.

Whether any of this can be proven might be argued but it has served a secondary purpose, making this man and his undead associates an important part of California lore.

HARRY WHEELER

(1876 - 1925)

Lawman

Harry Wheeler enlisted in the Arizona Rangers in 1903, eventually rising from the rank of private to captain of the organization.

Known for various shootouts with bad men and outlaws, he may have been one of the few "legitimate" Western personalities to earn the title of gunfighter. His ability as a deadly shot was well-known, as was his reputation for bravery beyond the bounds of normal duty, demonstrated most clearly in 1904 when he single-handedly stopped a hold-up in Willcox.

In 1909 the Arizona Rangers were disbanded and Wheeler sought other work. In 1912 he was elected sheriff of Cochise County, but his reign was a controversial one, especially concerning his methods of dealing with striking mine workers. He failed to gain popularity when, among other things, he ordered several strikers deported on cattle cars to New Mexico.

Although charged with "kidnapping" after this incident, the district attorney declined to prosecute. This didn't end the matter, for other legal action came, with Wheeler resigning his post, joining the Army, being sent east, then brought back to Arizona for trial, facing an assortment of charges along with his strike-breaker associates. All were eventually acquitted.

Wheeler died from pneumonia in Warren, Arizona at the age of 49.

HENRY WICKENBURG

(1819 - 1905)
Pioneer / Miner

Born Johannes Henricus Wickenburg, this Prussian migrated to America in 1847, in order to escape legal problems concerning a mining scandal.

For five years he lived in New York, then set sail for California via boat, where he resumed work as a miner. In 1862, he came to Arizona, discovering gold in June of the following year, in a location outside the foothills of Prescott, which he was to dub the Vulture Mine.

In 1866, a New York-based company bought the enterprise, but Wickenburg chose to remain near his discovery, rather than moving on as might have been predicted. He settled down in what would eventually become the town that carries his name.

For the rest of his life, Wickenburg remained a puzzling person, loved by some and hated by others. Reputed to be a great story-teller, he loved to speak of the episode where he alledgedly dared a trespasser to shoot him and he was subsequently shot!

Perhaps it was a sign of things to come, for in 1905 he was found dead, the victim of a bullet wound. Gossip was quick to spread that foul play was involved, possibly even a hired killing, but this remains speculative at best. Troubled by numerous ailments, it is more probable to think the 86-year-old prospector may have decided to end his own life.

The town of Wickenburg has since grown considerably, containing among other things, several dude ranches, museums, and a Jail Tree, where convicts were chained until they could be confined as no actual jail existed in the city. Old Wickenburg's grave, off of Howard Court Street, however, is seldom visited by tourists.

BILL WILLIAMS

(17?? - 1849)
Trapper / Explorer
Mountain Man

Little is known about the early life of "Old Bill" Williams, called that because he looked aged, even as a youth.

Reportedly, he came west as a missionary, bent on converting the Indians, but wound up a convert himself, to their more practical philosophy of living. From that moment on, he became an outdoorsman, learning numerous Indian languages, hunting, traveling, and scouting.

He was killed by a Ute war party on March 14, 1849, while camped out in southern Colorado. Beforehand, he had more than three decades of life in the wilderness to his credit, particularly in the Arizona-New Mexico area. The town of Williams, Arizona, carries his name to this day.

"Old Bill" was perhaps the greatest of all mountain men and early-day travelers of the frontier West. He was certainly one of the longest lasting and also one of the most eccentric. He talked, limped, and acted like an old-time Walter Brennan. For some unexplained reason, he chose to ride with the stirrups of his saddle so high, his knees stuck into the air, causing him to resemble a half-human frog atop a horse.

He was, however, a tough customer. Even in his final years he could run for miles without tiring, carry heavy equipment with ease, and drink endlessly without dropping or showing signs of sickness the following day. Although muskets and other firearms from his era were known to be both difficult to handle and inaccurate, he was reputed to be an unerring shot.

More incredible still is the realization that such stories were not the product of overblown myth.

BRIGHAM YOUNG

(1801 - 1877)
Pioneer / Religious Leader

Few realize that Brigham Young, born in Vermont, was a Methodist before converting to Mormonism.

Designated as an apostle in this religion in 1835, he spent a good deal of time traveling as a missionary for the cause. Wearing out his welcome in several states, he and a group of Mormons set off from Illinois in 1846, intending to find a "Promised Land" where they could settle peacefully.

Pausing briefly in Iowa and Nebraska, they came to the Salt Lake valley of Utah on July 24, 1847. Here they settled down, establishing a stronghold for Mormonism which exists to this very date. Continuing to be a figurehead for his religion, Young remained a busy man for the remainder of his life. He died in 1877, due to peritonitis stemming from an appendix attack.

Subscribing to the Mormon practice of polygamy, Young married more than 20 wives, with whom he fathered 57 children. Although tried for bigamy in 1871, he escaped conviction. He likewise kept busy with civil matters and a devotion to education.

He founded both the University of Deseret and the Brigham Young University, respectively. He took part in planning the construction of several Mormon Temples and also a transcontinental telegraph system, in addition to his many actions concerning the proselytizing of his faith.

To Mormons and non-Mormons alike, he remains the most famous face and name to come out of this religion, perhaps evern overshadowing its founder, Joseph Smith, with whom Young was personally acquainted.

JOSEPH ZIEGLER

(1855 ? - 1882)

Miner

Joseph Ziegler drifted into the Arizona area in the late 1870's, where he found work as a miner. He likewise proved that within Tombstone those who died by bullets were not always established gunfighters such as the Earp clan or the Clanton mob.

At times, ordinary men went for their weapons and became instant "gunfighters" as well, writing their own brief, but bloody sagas in the pages of history. Such was the case which brought him to a grave in Boot Hill.

Earlier in the day prior to his death, Ziegler got into a long-lasting argument with a fellow miner named Ed Williams while at work, over details which have since been forgotten with passing time. As evening came, Ziegler either thought the matter resolved or of so little consequence it was not worth troubling himself any further. The other party, though, had obviously different intentions and saw the topic of their disagreement worth pressing further, so far in fact, it was to be answered in lead.

As Ziegler walked behind an old ice house near the corner of Toughnut and Fifth Street, Williams stepped out of the shadows and shot him in the left breast. End of the line, as he died a few minutes afterward, spitting blood.

This was not the first or last time supposedly upright citizens would lose their tempers and resort to gunplay in Tombstone, which at one point grew to be so wild, President Arthur threatened to send in troops if order was not restored.

Index